ISBN: 9781290559119

Published by:
HardPress Publishing
8345 NW 66TH ST #2561
MIAMI FL 33166-2626

Email: info@hardpress.net
Web: http://www.hardpress.net

MY AFRICAN JOURNEY

MY AFRICAN JOURNEY

BY

THE RIGHT HON.
WINSTON SPENCER CHURCHILL, M.P.

AUTHOR OF "THE STORY OF THE MALAKAND FIELD FORCE,"
"THE RIVER WAR," "LONDON TO LADYSMITH," "IAN HAMILTON'S MARCH,"
"SAVROLA," "LIFE OF LORD RANDOLPH CHURCHILL"

WITH SIXTY-ONE ILLUSTRATIONS FROM PHOTOGRAPHS BY
THE AUTHOR AND LIEUTENANT-COLONEL GORDON
WILSON, AND THREE MAPS

TORONTO
WILLIAM BRIGGS
1909

RICHARD CLAY & SONS, LIMITED,
BREAD STREET HILL, E.C., AND
BUNGAY, SUFFOLK.

PREFACE

In so far as the collection of information is concerned, the advantages of travel may often be over-stated. So much has been written, so many facts are upon record about every country, even the most remote, that a judicious and persevering study of existing materials would no doubt enable a reader to fill himself with knowledge almost to repletion without leaving his chair. But for the formation of opinion, for the stirring and enlivenment of thought, and for the discernment of colour and proportion, the gifts of travel, especially of travel on foot, are priceless. It was with the design and in the hope of securing such prizes, that I undertook last year the pilgrimage of which these pages give account. I cannot tell whether I have succeeded in winning them; and still less whether, if won, they are transferable. I therefore view these letters with a modest eye. They were written mainly in long hot Uganda afternoons, after the day's march was done. The larger portion has already appeared in the *Strand Magazine*, and what has been added was necessary to complete the story.

They present a continuous narrative of the lighter side of what was to me a very delightful and inspiring journey; and it is in the hope that they may vivify and fortify the interest of the British people in the wonderful estates they have recently acquired in the north-eastern quarter of Africa, that I offer them in a connected form to the indulgence of the public.

WINSTON SPENCER CHURCHILL

London, 1908.

CONTENTS

CHAPTER I

CONTENTS

ILLUSTRATIONS

ILLUSTRATIONS

ILLUSTRATIONS xiii

MAPS

CHAPTER I

THE aspect of Mombasa as she rises from the sea and clothes herself with form and colour at the swift approach of the ship is alluring and even delicious. But to appreciate all these charms the traveller should come from the North. He should see the hot stones of Malta, baking and glistening on a steel-blue Mediterranean. He should visit the Island of Cyprus before the autumn rains have revived the soil, when the Messaoria Plain is one broad wilderness of dust, when every tree—be it only a thorn-bush—is an heirloom, and every drop of water is a jewel. He should walk for two hours at midday in the streets of Port Said. He should thread the long red furrow of the Suez Canal, and swelter through the trough of the Red Sea. He should pass a day among the cinders of Aden, and a week among the scorched rocks and stones of Northern Somaliland; and then, after five days of open sea, his eye and mind will be prepared to salute with feelings of grateful delight these shores of vivid and exuberant green.   On every side is vegetation, moist, tumultuous, and varied.   Great trees, clad in dense foliage, shrouded in creepers, springing from beds of verdure, thrust themselves through the undergrowth ; palms laced together by flowering trailers ; every kind of tropical plant that lives by rain and sunshine ; high waving grass, brilliant patches of purple bougainvillea, and in the midst, dotted about, scarcely keeping their heads above the fertile flood of Nature, the red-roofed houses of the town and port of Mombasa.

The vessel follows a channel twisting away between high bluffs, and finds a secure anchorage, land-locked, in forty feet of water at a stone's throw from the shore.   Here we are arrived at the gate of British East Africa ; and more, at the outlet and debouchment of all the trade of all the countries that lap the Victoria and Albert Lakes and the head-waters of the Nile.   Along the pier now being built at Kilindini, the harbour of Mombasa Island, must flow, at any rate for ·many years, the main stream of East and Central African com-

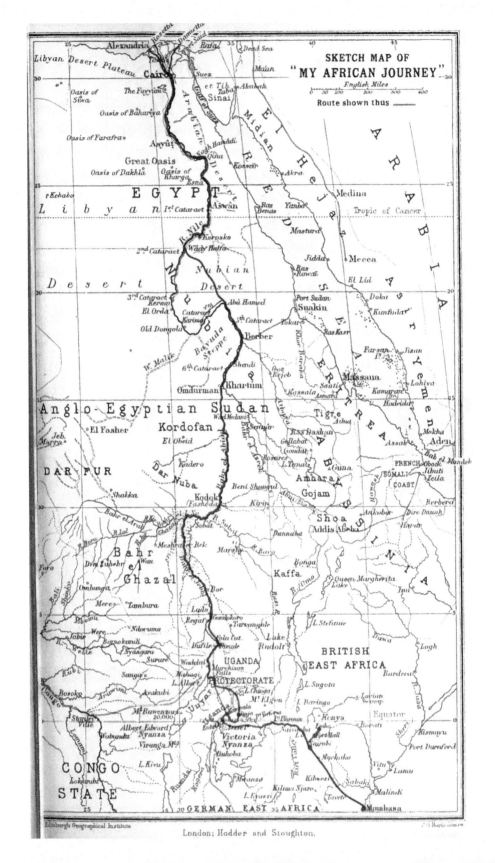

Edinburgh Geographical Institute

SKETCH MAP OF
"MY AFRICAN JOURNEY"

English Miles

0   50 100   200   300   400

Route shown thus

London: Hodder and Stoughton.

merce. Whatever may be the produce which civilized government and enterprise will draw from the enormous territories between Southern Abyssinia and Lake Tanganyika, between Lake Rudolf and Ruenzori, as far west as the head-streams of the Congo, as far north as the Lado enclave ; whatever may be the needs and demands of the numerous populations comprised within those limits, it is along the unpretentious jetty of Kilindini that the whole traffic must pass.

For Kilindini (or Mombasa, as I may be permitted to call it) is the starting-point of one of the most romantic and most wonderful railways in the world. The two iron streaks of rail that wind away among the hills and foliage of Mombasa Island do not break their smooth monotony until, after piercing Equatorial forests, stretching across immense prairies, and climbing almost to the level of the European snow-line, they pause—and that only for a time—upon the edges of the Great Lake. And thus is made a sure, swift road along which the white man and all that he brings with him, for good or ill, may penetrate into the heart of Africa as easily and safely as he may travel from London to Vienna.

Short has been the life, many the vicissitudes, of the Uganda Railway. The adventurous enterprise of a Liberal Government, it
was soon exposed, disowned, to the merciless
criticism of its parents. Adopted as a cherished
foundling by the Conservative party, it almost
perished from mismanagement in their hands.
Nearly ten thousand pounds a mile were expended upon its construction; and so eager
were all parties to be done with it and its
expense that, instead of pursuing its proper
and natural route across the plateau to the
deep waters of Port Victoria, it fell by the
way into the shallow gulf of Kavirondo, lucky
to get so far. It is easy to censure, it is impossible not to criticize, the administrative
mistakes and miscalculations which tarnished
and nearly marred a brilliant conception. But
it is still more easy, as one traverses in forty-
eight hours countries which ten years ago
would have baffled the toilsome marches of
many weeks, to underrate the difficulties in
which unavoidable ignorance and astonishing
conditions plunged the pioneers. The British
art of " muddling through " is here seen in one
of its finest expositions. Through everything
—through the forests, through the ravines,

through troops of marauding lions, through famine, through war, through five years of excoriating Parliamentary debate, muddled and marched the railway ; and here at last, in some more or less effective fashion, is it arrived at its goal. Other nations project Central African railways as lightly and as easily as they lay down naval programmes ; but here is a railway, like the British Fleet, " in being "— not a paper plan or an airy dream, but an iron fact grinding along through the jungle and the plain, waking with its whistles the silences of the Nyanza, and startling the tribes out of their primordial nakedness with " Americani " piece goods *made in Lancashire.*

Let us, then, without waiting in Mombasa longer than is necessary to wish it well and to admire the fertility and promise of the coastal region, ascend this railway from the sea to the lake. And first, what a road it is ! Everything is in apple-pie order. The track is smoothed and weeded and ballasted as if it were the London and North-Western. Every telegraph-post has its number ; every mile, every hundred yards, every change of gradient has its mark ; not in soft wood, to feed the white ant, but in hard, well-painted iron.

Constant labour has steadily improved the grades and curves of the permanent-way, and the train—one of those comfortable, practical Indian trains—rolls along as evenly as upon a European line.

Nor should it be supposed that this high standard of maintenance is not warranted by the present financial position of the line. The Uganda Railway is already doing what it was never expected within any reasonable period to do. It is paying its way. It is beginning to yield a profit—albeit a small profit—upon its capital charge. Projected solely as a political railway to reach Uganda, and to secure British predominance upon the Upper Nile, it has already achieved a commercial value. Instead of the annual deficits upon working expenses which were regularly anticipated by those most competent to judge, there is already a substantial profit of nearly eighty thousand pounds a year. And this is but the beginning, and an imperfect beginning; for at present the line is only a trunk, without its necessary limbs and feeders, without its deep-water head at Kilindini, without its full tale of steamers on the lake; above all, without its natural and necessary extension to the Albert Nyanza.

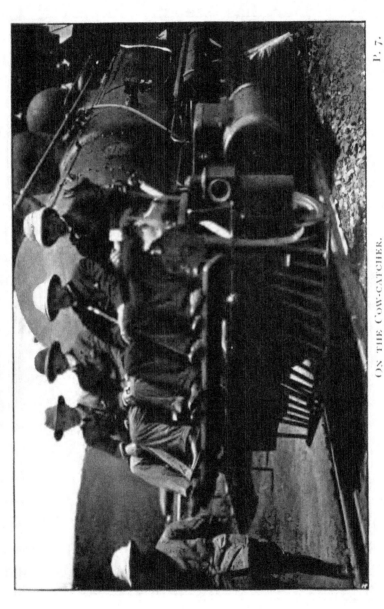

ON THE COW-CATCHER.

(Mr. Currie, Mr. Marsh, Col. Wilson, Sir J. Hayes-Sadler Mr. Churchill.)

P. 7.

We may divide the journey into four main stages—the jungles, the plains, the mountains, and the lake, for the lake is an essential part of the railway, and a natural and inexpensive extension to its length. In the early morning, then, we start from Mombasa Station, taking our places upon an ordinary garden seat fastened on to the cow-catcher of the engine, from which position the whole country can be seen. For a quarter of an hour we are still upon Mombasa Island, and then the train, crossing the intervening channel by a long iron bridge, addresses itself in earnest to the continent of Africa. Into these vast regions the line winds perseveringly upon a stiff up-grade, and the land unfolds itself ridge after ridge and valley after valley, till soon, with one farewell glance at the sea and at the fighting-tops of His Majesty's ship *Venus* rising queerly amid the palms, we are embraced and engulfed completely. All day long the train runs upward and westward, through broken and undulating ground clad and encumbered with superabundant vegetation. Beautiful birds and butterflies fly from tree to tree and flower to flower. Deep, ragged gorges, filled by streams in flood, open out far below us through glades of palms and creeper-covered trees. Here and there, at intervals, which will become shorter every year, are plantations of rubber, fibre, and cotton, the beginnings of those inexhaustible supplies which will one day meet the yet unmeasured demand of Europe for those indispensable commodities. Every few miles are little trim stations, with their water-tanks, signals, ticket-offices, and flower-beds complete and all of a pattern, backed by impenetrable bush. In brief one slender thread of scientific civilization, of order, authority, and arrangement, drawn across the primeval chaos of the world.

In the evening a cooler, crisper air is blowing. The humid coast lands, with their glories and their fevers, have been left behind. At an altitude of four thousand feet we begin to laugh at the Equator. The jungle becomes forest, not less luxuriant, but distinctly different in character. The olive replaces the palm. The whole aspect of the land is more friendly, more familiar, and no less fertile. After Makindu Station the forest ceases. The traveller enters upon a region of grass. Immense fields of green pasture, withered and whitened at this season by waiting for the rains, intersected by streams and watercourses densely wooded with dark, fir-looking trees and gorse-looking scrub, and relieved by bold upstanding bluffs and ridges, comprise the new panorama. And here is presented the wonderful and unique spectacle which the Uganda Railway offers to the European. *The plains are crowded with wild animals.* From the windows of the carriage the whole zoological gardens can be seen disporting itself. Herds of antelope and gazelle, troops of zebras —sometimes four or five hundred together— watch the train pass with placid assurance, or scamper a hundred yards farther away, and turn again. Many are quite close to the line. With field-glasses one can see that it is the same everywhere, and can distinguish long files of black wildebeeste and herds of red kongoni—the hartebeeste of South Africa— and wild ostriches walking sedately in twos and threes, and every kind of small deer and gazelle. The zebras come close enough for their stripes to be admired with the naked eye.

We have arrived at Simba, " The Place of Lions," and there is no reason why the passengers should not see one, or even half-a-dozen, stalking across the plain, respectfully

observed by lesser beasts.   Indeed, in the
early days it was the custom to stop and sally
out upon the royal vermin whenever met with,
and many the lion that has been carried back
to the tender in triumph before the guard, or
driver, or any one else could think of time-
tables or the block system, or the other in-
convenient restrictions of a regular service.
Farther up the line, in the twilight of the
evening, we saw, not a hundred yards away,
a dozen giraffes lollopping off among scattered
trees, and at Nakuru six yellow lions walked
in leisurely mood across the rails in broad
daylight.   Only the rhinoceros is absent, or
rarely seen, and after one of his species had
measured his strength, unsuccessfully, against
an engine, he has confined himself morosely
to the river-beds and to the undisturbed
solitudes which, at a distance of two or
three miles, everywhere engulf the Uganda
Railway.

Our carriage stopped upon a siding at Simba
Station for three days, in order that we might
more closely examine the local fauna.   One of
the best ways of shooting game in this part of
the world, and certainly the easiest, is to get a
trolly and run up and down the line.   The

animals are so used to the passage of trains and natives along the one great highway that they do not, as a rule, take much notice, unless the train or trolly stops, when their suspicions are at once aroused. The sportsmen should, therefore, slip off without allowing the vehicle or the rest of the party to stop, even for a moment; and in this way he will frequently find himself within two hundred and fifty or three hundred yards of his quarry, when the result will be governed solely by his skill, or want of skill, with the rifle.

There is another method, which we tried on the second day in the hopes of finding a water-buck, and that is, to prowl about among the trees and undergrowth of the river-bed. In a few minutes one may bury oneself in the wildest and savagest kind of forest. The air becomes still and hot. The sun seems in an instant to assert his just prerogative. The heat glitters over the open spaces of dry sand and pools of water. High grass, huge boulders, tangled vegetation, multitudes of thorn-bushes, obstruct the march, and the ground itself is scarped and guttered by the rains into the strangest formations. Around you, breast-high, shoulder-high, overhead, rises the African jungle. There is a brooding silence, broken only by the cry of a bird, or the scolding bark of baboons, and the crunching of one's own feet on the crumbling soil. We enter the haunt of the wild beasts; their tracks, their traces, the remnants of their repasts, are easily and frequently discovered. Here a lion has passed since the morning. There a rhinoceros has certainly been within the hour—perhaps within ten minutes. We creep and scramble through the game paths, anxiously, rifles at full cock, not knowing what each turn or step may reveal. The wind, when it blows at all, blows fitfully, now from this quarter, now from that ; so that one can never be certain that it will not betray the intruder in these grim domains to the beast he seeks, or to some other, less welcome, before he sees him. At length, after two hours' scramble and scrape, we emerge breathless, as from another world, half astonished to find ourselves within a quarter of a mile of the railway line, with its trolly, luncheon, soda-water, ice, etc.

But if one would seek the rhinoceros in his open pastures, it is necessary to go farther afield ; and accordingly we started the next morning, while the stars were still shining, to

THE RHINOCEROS AT SIMBA.

P. 12

tramp over the ridges and hills which shut in the railway, and overlook remoter plains and valleys beyond. The grass grows high from ground honeycombed with holes and heaped with lava boulders, and it was daylight before we had stumbled our way to a spur commanding a wide view. Here we halted to search the country with field-glasses, and to brush off the ticks—detestable insects which infest all the resorts of the game in innumerable swarms, ready to spread any poison among the farmers' cattle. The glass disclosed nothing of consequence. Zebra, wildebeeste, and kongoni were to be seen in troops and herds, scattered near and far over the plains, but never a rhinoceros! So we trudged on, meaning to make a wide circle. For an hour we found nothing, and then, just as we were thinking of turning homewards before the sun should get his full power, three beautiful oryx, great, dark-coloured antelope with very long, corrugated horns, walked over the next brow on their way to water. Forthwith we set off in pursuit, crouching and creeping along the valley, and hoping to intercept them at the stream. Two passed safely over before we could reach our point. The third, seeing us, turned back and disappeared over the hill, where, a quarter of an hour later, he was stalked and wounded.

It is always the wounded beast that leads the hunter into adventures. Till the quarry is hit every one walks delicately, avoids going the windward side of unexplored coverts, skirts a reed-bed cautiously, notices a convenient tree, looks often this way and that. But once the prize is almost within reach, you scramble along after it as fast as your legs will carry you, and never trouble about remoter contingencies, be they what they may. Our oryx led us a mile or more over rocky slopes, always promising and never giving a good chance for a shot, until at last he drew us round the shoulder of a hill—and there, abruptly, was the rhinoceros. The impression was extraordinary. A wide plain of white, withered grass stretched away to low hills broken with rocks. The rhinoceros stood in the middle of this plain, about five hundred yards away, in jet-black silhouette; not a twentieth-century animal at all, but an odd, grim straggler from the Stone Age. He was grazing placidly, and above him the vast snow dome of Kilimanjaro towered up in the clear air of morning to complete a scene unaltered since the dawn of the world.

The manner of killing a rhinoceros in the open is crudely simple. It is thought well usually to select the neighbourhood of a good tree, *where one can be found*, as the centre of the encounter. If no tree is available, you walk up as near as possible to him from any side except the windward, and then shoot him in the head or the heart. If you hit a vital spot, as sometimes happens, he falls. If you hit him anywhere else, he charges blindly and furiously in your direction, and you shoot him again, or not, as the case may be.

Bearing all this carefully in mind, we started out to do battle with Behemoth. We had advanced perhaps two hundred yards towards him, when a cry from one of the natives arrested us. We looked sharply to the right. There, not a hundred and fifty paces distant, under the shade of a few small trees, stood two other monsters. In a few more steps we should have tainted their wind and brought them up with a rush; and suppose this had happened, when perhaps we were already compromised with our first friend, and had him wounded and furious on our hands! Luckily

warned in time, to creep back to the shoulder
of the hill, to skirt its crest, and to emerge
a hundred and twenty yards from this new
objective was the work of a few minutes. We
hurriedly agree to kill one first before touch-
ing the other. At such a range it is easy to
hit so great a target ; but the bull's-eye is small.
I fired. The thud of a bullet which strikes
with an impact of a ton and a quarter, tearing
through hide and muscle and bone with the
hideous energy of cordite, came back distinctly.
The large rhinoceros started, stumbled, turned
directly towards the sound and the blow, and
then bore straight down upon us in a peculiar
trot, nearly as fast as a horse's gallop, with an
activity surprising in so huge a beast, and
instinct with unmistakable purpose.

Great is the moral effect of a foe who advances. Everybody fired. Still the ponderous
brute came on, as if he were invulnerable ; as if
he were an engine, or some great steam barge
impervious to bullets, insensible to pain or fear.
Thirty seconds more, and he will close. An
impalpable curtain seems to roll itself up in
the mind, revealing a mental picture, strangely
lighted, yet very still, where objects have new
values, and where a patch of white grass in the

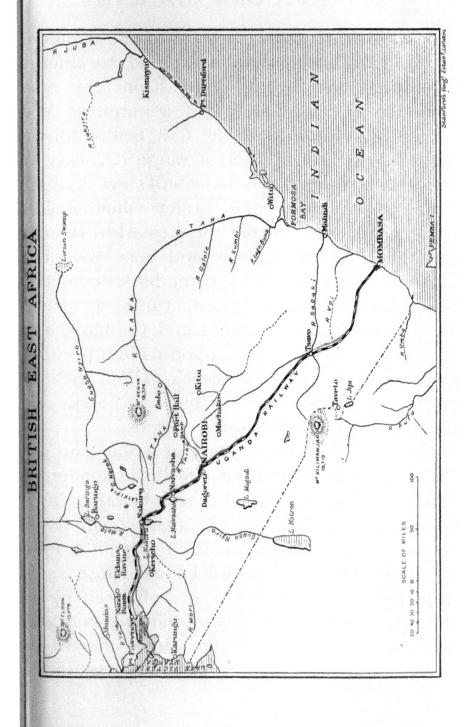

foreground, four or five yards away, seems to possess astonishing significance. It is there that the last two shots that yet remain before the resources of civilization are exhausted must be fired. There is time to reflect with some detachment that, after all, we were the aggressors; we it is who have forced the conflict by an unprovoked assault with murderous intent upon a peaceful herbivore; that if there is such a thing as right and wrong between man and beast—and who shall say there is not? —right is plainly on his side; there is time for this before I perceive that, stunned and dazed by the frightful concussions of modern firearms, he has swerved sharp to the right, and is now moving across our front, broadside on, at the same swift trot. More firing, and as I reload some one says he is down, and I fire instead at his smaller companion, already some distance off upon the plain. But one rhinoceros hunt is like another, except in its details, and I will not occupy the reader with the account of this new pursuit and death. Suffice it to say that, in all the elements of neurotic experience, such an encounter seems to me fully equal to half an hour's brisk skirmish at six or seven hundred yards—and with an important addition.

2

In war there is a cause, there is duty, there is the hope of glory, for who can tell what may not be won before night ?　But here at the end is only a hide, a horn, and a carcase, over which the vultures have already begun to wheel.

CHAPTER II

AROUND MOUNT KENYA

THE town of Nairobi, the capital of the East Africa Protectorate, stands on the base of wooded hills at the three hundred and twenty-seventh mile of the railroad. Originally chosen as a convenient place for assembling the extensive depots and shops necessary to the construction and maintenance of the railway, it enjoys no advantages as a residential site. The ground on which the town is built is low and swampy. The supply of water is indifferent, and the situation generally unhealthy. A mile farther on, however, upon the rising ground a finer position could have been found, and this quarter is already being occupied sparsely by Government buildings, hospitals, and barracks. It is now too late to change, and thus lack of foresight and of a comprehensive view leaves its permanent imprint upon the countenance of a new country.

19

Our train traverses the Athi plains, more crowded perhaps with game than any other part of the line, and approaches swiftly the long rows of one-storeyed tin houses which constitute the town. Nairobi is a typical South African township. It might be Pietermaritzburg or Ladysmith of twenty years ago, before blue gum-trees and stone buildings had waxed and multiplied. In its present stage perhaps it resembles Buluwayo most. The population is also South African in its character and proportions. There are five hundred and eighty whites, three thousand one hundred Indians, and ten thousand five hundred and fifty African natives. The shops and stores are, however, much more considerable than these figures would appear to warrant, and are fully capable of supplying the varied needs of settlers and planters over a wide area. Nairobi is also the headquarters of a brigade of the King's African Rifles, the central office and depot of the Uganda Railway, and the seat of the Administration, with its numerous official *personnel.* The dinner of the Colonists' Association, to which I was invited, afforded the familiar, yet in Central Africa not unimpressive, spectacle of long rows of gentlemen

GUARD OF HONOUR, KING'S AFRICAN RIFLES.

P. 20.

in evening dress; while the ball given by the
Governor to celebrate the King's birthday
revealed a company gay with uniforms, and
ladies in pretty dresses, assembled upon a spot
where scarcely ten years before lions hunted
undisturbed.

Every white man in Nairobi is a politician;
and most of them are leaders of parties. One
would scarcely believe it possible, that a centre
so new should be able to develop so many
divergent and conflicting interests, or that a
community so small should be able to give to
each such vigorous and even vehement expression. There are already in miniature all the
elements of keen political and racial discord,
all the materials for hot and acrimonious
debate. The white man *versus* the black; the
Indian *versus* both; the settler as against the
planter; the town contrasted with the country;
the official class against the unofficial; the
coast and the highlands; the railway administration and the Protectorate generally; the
King's African Rifles and the East Africa
Protectorate Police; all these different points
of view, naturally arising, honestly adopted,
tenaciously held, and not yet reconciled into
any harmonious general conception, confront

the visitor in perplexing disarray. Nor will he be wise to choose his part with any hurry. It is better to see something of the country, of its quality and extent, of its promises and forfeits, of its realities and illusions, before endeavouring to form even a provisional opinion.

The snow-clad peak of Mount Kenya, a hundred miles away, can on a clear morning be easily seen from the slopes above Nairobi— a sharp, serrated summit veined with gleaming white. A road—passable, albeit unmetalled, for wagons and even a motor-car — runs thitherward by Fort Hall and across the Tana River. On the way there is much to see. A wild, ragged-looking, but fertile region, swelling into successive undulations and intersected by numerous gorges whose streams are shaded by fine trees, unfolds itself to the eye. Scattered about upon spacious estates of many thousand acres are a score or two of colonists, each gradually making himself a home and a living in his own way. One raises stock; another plants coffee, which grows so exuberantly in this generous soil as to threaten the speedy exhaustion of the plant. Here are ostriches, sheep, and cattle standing placidly

Breakdown on the way to Thika Camp.

P. 22.

together in one drove under the guardianship of a native child of eleven. There is a complete dairy farm, admirably equipped. One of the streams has been dammed effectively, and turbines are already in position to light Nairobi with electricity. Upon the banks of another there is talk of building an hotel.

At one place I found a family of good people from Hightown, Manchester, grappling courageously with an enormous tract of ten thousand acres. Hard by, an old Boer, who has trekked the length of Africa to avoid the British flag, sits smoking stolidly by his grass house, reconciled to British rule at last by a few months' experience of paternal government in a neighbouring Protectorate. He has few cattle and less cash, but he holds decided views as to the whereabouts of lions; there, moreover, stands the heavy tilted wagon of the Great Trek—an ark of refuge when all else fails; and for the rest there is plenty of game, few people, and the family grows from year to year. In short, one sees a sparse, heterogeneous population engaged in varied labours; but everywhere hard work, straitened resources, hopes persisting through many dis-

appointments, stout hospitable hearts, and
the beginnings, at any rate, of progress.

A camp has been prepared for me in a
very beautiful spot at the juncture of the
Chania and Thika rivers. Tents are pitched
and grass shelters are erected in a smooth
meadow. Southwards, a hundred yards away,
a fine waterfall plunges downwards over
enormous boulders amid tall, interlacing trees.
The muffled roar of another rises from a deep
ravine an equal distance to the north; and
the Philistine computes, with a frown, four
thousand horse-power expending itself upon
the picturesque.

Nothing causes the East African colonist
more genuine concern than that his guest should
not have been provided with a lion. The
knowledge preys upon his mind until it becomes a veritable obsession. · He feels some
deep reproach is laid upon his own hospitality
and the reputation of his adopted country.
How to find, and, having found, to kill, a lion
is the unvarying theme of conversation; and
every place and every journey is judged by a
simple standard—" lions or no lions." At
the Thika camp, then, several gentlemen,
accomplished in this important sport, have

SHOOTING PARTY AT THIKA CAMP.

From left to right—Capt. Sadler, Major Riddell, Mr. Marsh, Marquis Gandolfi-Hornyold, Hon. K. Dundas
Mr. Percival, Mr. Churchill, Mr. D. J. Wilson.

P. 24.

come together with ponies, rifles, Somalis, and all the other accessories. Some zebras and kongoni have been killed and left lying in likely-looking places to attract the lions; and at 4 a.m., rain or shine, we are to go and look for them.

The young Englishman, be he officer or settler in the East African Highlands, cuts a hardy figure. His clothes are few and far between: a sun hat, a brown flannel shirt with sleeves cut above the elbow and open to the chest, a pair of thin khaki knicker-bockers cut short five inches—*at least*—above the knee, boots, and a pair of putties comprise the whole attire. Nothing else is worn. The skin, exposed to sun, thorns, and insects, becomes almost as dark as that of the natives, and so hardened that it is nothing to ride all day with bare knees on the saddle; a truly Spartan discipline from which at least the visitor may be excused.

This is the way in which they hunt lions. First find the lion, lured to a kill, driven from a reed-bed, or kicked up incontinently by the way. Once viewed he must never be lost sight of for a moment. Mounted on ponies of more or less approved fidelity, three or four daring Britons or Somalis gallop after him, as in India they ride the pig—that is to say, 'neck or nothing—across rocks, holes, tussocks, nullahs, through high grass, thorn scrub, undergrowth, turning him, shepherding him, heading him this way and that until he is brought to bay. For his part the lion is no seeker of quarrels; he is often described in accents of contempt. His object throughout is to save his skin. If, being unarmed, you meet six or seven lions unexpectedly, all you need do—according to my information—is to speak to them sternly and they will slink away, while you throw a few stones at them to hurry them up. All the highest authorities recommend this.

But when pursued from place to place, chased hither and thither by the wheeling horsemen, the naturally mild disposition of the lion becomes embittered. First he begins to growl and roar at his enemies, in order to terrify them, and make them leave him in peace. Then he darts little short charges at them. Finally, when every attempt at peaceful persuasion has failed, he pulls up abruptly and offers battle. Once he has done this, he will run no more. He means to fight,

and to fight to the death.   He means to
charge home; and when a lion, maddened
with the agony of a bullet-wound, distressed
by long and hard pursuit, or, most of all, a
lioness in defence of her cubs, is definitely
committed to the charge, death is the only
possible conclusion.   Broken limbs, broken
jaws, a body raked from end to end, lungs
pierced through and through, entrails torn
and protruding—none of these count.   It
must be death—instant and utter—for the
lion, or down goes the man, mauled by septic
claws and fetid teeth, crushed and crunched,
and poisoned afterwards to make doubly sure.
Such are the habits of this cowardly and
wicked animal.

It is at the stage when the lion has been
determinedly "bayed" that the sportsman
from London is usually introduced upon the
scene.   He has, we may imagine, followed
the riders as fast as the inequalities of the
ground, his own want of training, and the
burden of a heavy rifle will allow him.   He
arrives at the spot where the lion is cornered
in much the same manner as the matador
enters the arena, the others standing aside
deferentially, ready to aid him or divert the

lion.   If his bullet kills, he is, no doubt, justly
proud.   If it only wounds, the lion charges the
nearest horseman.   For forty yards the charge
of a lion is swifter than the gallop of a racehorse.
The riders, therefore, usually avoid waiting
within that distance.   But sometimes they do
not ; or sometimes the lion sees the man who
has shot him ; or sometimes all sorts of things
happen which make good stories—afterwards.

After this general description no particular
example is required, and the reader need not
be disappointed to learn that our lion escaped
what, no doubt, would have been his certain
destruction by the breaking of a single link in
the regular chain of circumstances.   He was
not found upon the kill.   His place was taken
by a filthy hyena, and it was not until we had
beaten thoroughly for two hours more than
three miles of reed-bed that we saw him—a
splendid great yellow cat, looking as big as a
bullock—bounding away up the opposite hill.
Off started our riders like falcons ; but alas !—
if "alas !" is the proper word—a deep and
impassable nullah intervened, necessitating
large circuits and long delays ; so that the
lion got clean away out of sight of all men,
and we were reduced to the slow and tedious

THE BANDA AT THIKA CAMP.

COLONEL WILSON'S LION.　　　　　P. 28.

process of tracking him footprint by footprint through waving grass, breast-high, hour after hour, always expecting to tread on his tail, and always—disappointed!

In the afternoon I had to ride to Fort Hall, where there was to be a great gathering of Kikuyu chiefs and thousands of their warriors and women. The country is much the same as that traversed on the previous day, but greener, smoother, and more pleasant-looking. Fort Hall is not a fort in any military sense, but the Commissioner's house with a ditch round it, a jail, a few houses, and an Indian bazaar. The station is hardly well selected, being perched up on a hill out of the reach of any railway—and unhealthy nevertheless. The whole place was crowded with natives in their most highly ornamented and elaborate nudity, waiting for the war-dance.

This ceremony was performed the next morning. Long before daylight the beating of drums, the blowing of horns, and the rhythm of loud, yet not altogether un-melodious chanting awakened the weariest sleeper; and when, at eight o'clock the *indaba* began, the whole space in front of the fort was densely packed with naked, painted, plumed, and gyrating humanity, which seethed continually to and fro, and divided from time to time as particular chiefs advanced with their followers, or as gifts of struggling sheep and bulls were brought forward. In his war dress the Kikuyu, and, still more, the Masai warrior, is a striking, if not impressive, figure. His hair and body are smeared with the red earth of his native land, compounded into a pigment by mixture with the slimy juice of the castor-oil plant, which abounds. Fantastic head-dresses, some of ostrich feathers, others of metal or leather ; armlets and leglets of twisted wire ; stripes of white clay rubbed across the red pigment ; here and there an old pot-hat or some European garment, incongruously contrasted with leopard-skins and bulls' horns ; broad, painted cow-hide shields, and spears with soft iron blades nearly four feet long, complete a grotesque and indecorous picture. Still, there is a sleek grace about these active forms—bronze statues but for their frippery—which defeats all their own efforts to make themselves hideous. The chiefs, however, succeed in reducing themselves to regular guys. Any old, cast-off khaki jacket or tattered pair of trousers ; any fragment of

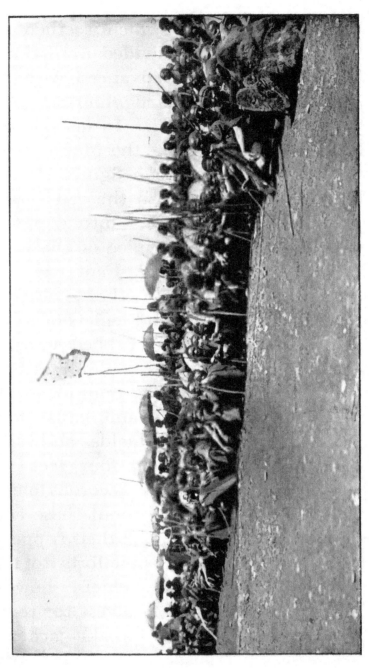

"DURBAR" AT KIAMBU.

P. 30.

weather-stained uniform, a battered sun-helmet
with a feather stuck lamely into the top of it,
a ragged umbrella, is sufficient to induce them
to abandon the ostrich plume and the leopard-
skin kaross.   Among their warriors in ancient
gear they look ridiculous and insignificant—
more like the commonest kind of native sweeper
than the hereditary rulers of some powerful and
numerous tribe.

It is unquestionably an advantage that the
East African negro should develop a taste for
civilized attire.   In no more useful and inno-
cent direction could his wants be multiplied
and his desires excited, and it is by this
process of assimilation that his life will
gradually be made more complicated, more
varied, less crudely animal, and himself raised
to a higher level of economic utility. ' But it
would surely be worth while to organize and
guide this new motive force within graceful
and appropriate limits.   A Government runs
risks when it intrudes upon the domain of
fashion ; but when a veritable abyss of knowledge and science separates the rulers from the
ruled, when authority is dealing with a native
race still plunged in its primary squalour, without religion, without clothes, without morals,

but willing to emerge and capable of emerging, such risks may fairly be accepted ; and the Government might well prescribe or present suitable robes for ceremonial occasions to the chiefs, and gradually encourage, and more gradually still enforce, their adoption throughout the population.

After the dance it had been arranged that I should go as far as the bank of the Tana River to see the view of Mount Kenya, and then return to the Thika camp before night. But when the whole splendid panorama of the trans-Tana country opened upon us, I could not bring myself to stop short of the promised land ; and, casting away material cares of luncheon and baggage, I decided to ride through to Embo, twenty-eight miles from Fort Hall, and our most advanced post in this direction. We crossed the Tana by a ferry which travels along a rope under the impulsion of the current. The ponies swam the deep, strong, sixty-yard stream of turbulent red water. On the farther bank the country is really magnificent in quality and aspect. The centre of the picture is always Mount Kenya ; but there never was a mountain which made so little of its height. It rises by long gentle slopes, more like a swelling of ground than a peak, from an immense upland plain, and so gradual is the acclivity that, but for the sudden outcrop of snow-clad rock which crowns the summit, no one would believe it over eighteen thousand feet high. It is its gradual rise that imparts so great a value to this noble mountain ; for about its enormous base and upon its slopes, traversed by hundreds of streams of clear perennial water, there grows, or may grow, in successive, concentric belts, every kind of crop and forest known in the world, from the Equator to the Arctic Circle. The landscape is superb. In beauty, in fertility, in verdure, in the coolness of the air, in the abundance of running water, in its rich red soil, in the variety of its vegetation, the scenery about Kenya far surpasses anything I have ever seen in India or South Africa, and challenges comparison with the fairest countries of Europe. Indeed, looking at it with an eye fresh from Italy, I was most powerfully reminded of the upper valleys of the Po.

We rode on all day through this delicious country, along a well-kept native road, smooth enough for a bicycle, except where it crossed

3

stream after stream on primitive bridges. On every side the soil was cultivated and covered with the crops of a large and industrious population. It is only a year since regular control was established beyond the Tana, not without some bloodshed, by a small military expedition. Yet so peaceful are the tribes—now that their intertribal fighting has been stopped—that white officers ride freely about among their villages without even carrying a pistol. All the natives met with on the road were armed with sword and spear, and all offered us their customary salutations, while many came up smiling and holding out long, moist, delicate-looking hands for me to shake, till I had quite enough of it. Indeed, the only dangers of the road appear to be from the buffaloes which infest the country, and after nightfall place the traveller in real peril. We were very glad for this reason, and also because we had eaten nothing but a banana each since early morning, to see at last on the top of the next hill the buildings of Embo just as the sun sank beneath the horizon.

Embo is a model station, only five months old—one small, three-roomed house for the District Commissioner, one for the military

officer, an office, and a tiny jail, all in good
dressed stone ; two Indian shops in corrugated
iron ; and seven or eight long rows of beehive
grass huts for a hundred and fifty soldiers and
police.   Two young white officers—a civilian
and a soldier — preside from this centre of
authority, far from the telegraph, over the
peace and order of an area as large as an
English county, and regulate the conduct and
fortunes of some seventy-five thousand natives,
who have never previously known or acknow-
ledged any law but violence or terror.   They
were uncommonly surprised to see four horsemen come riding up the zigzag path to their
dwelling ; but their astonishment was no bar
to their hospitality, and we were soon rewarded
for our journey and our fasting in most excellent fashion.

I had just time before the darkness flooded
the land and blotted out the mighty mountain
and its wreaths of fire-tipped cloud to walk
round this station.   The jail consisted of a
single room, barred and bolted.   Inside not a
prisoner was to be seen.   I inquired where
they were, and was shown two little groups
seated round fires in the open.   They were
chained together by a light running chain, and

after a hard day's miscellaneous work about the station they chatted peacefully as they cooked and ate their evening meal. The prison was only their shelter for the night —primitive arrangements, no doubt, but are they more barbarous than the hideous, long-drawn precision of an English convict establishment ?

The African protectorates now administered by the Colonial Office afford rare scope for the abilities of earnest and intelligent youth. A man of twenty-five may easily find himself ruling a large tract of country and a numerous population. The Government is too newly established to have developed the highly centralized and closely knit—perhaps too closely knit — hierarchy and control of the Indian system. It is far too poor to afford a complete Administration. The District Commissioner must judge for himself, and be judged upon his actions. Very often—for tropical diseases make many gaps in the ranks, and men must often return to England to recruit their health —the officer is not a District Commissioner at all, but a junior acting in his stead or in some one's stead, sometimes for a year or more. To him there come day by day the natives of the district with all their troubles, disputes, and intrigues. Their growing appreciation of the impartial justice of the tribunal leads them increasingly to carry all sorts of cases to the District Commissioner's Court. When they are ill they come and ask for medicine. When they are wounded in their quarrels it is to the white man they go to have the injuries dressed. Disease and accident have to be combated without professional skill. Courts of justice and forms of legality must be maintained without lawyers. Taxes have to be collected by personal influence. Peace has to be kept with only a shadow of force.

All these great opportunities of high service, and many others, are often and daily placed within the reach of men in their twenties—on the whole with admirable results. It was most pleasant to hear with what comprehension and sympathy the officers of the East Africa Protectorate speak about their work ; and how they regard themselves as the guardians of native interests and native rights against those who only care about exploiting the country and its people. No one can travel even for a little while among the Kikuyu tribes without acquiring a liking for these light-hearted, tractable, if brutish

children, or without feeling that they are
capable of being instructed and raised from
their present degradation. There are more
than four million aboriginals in East Africa
alone. Their care imposes a grave, and I think
an inalienable, responsibility upon the British
Government. It will be an ill day for these
native races when their fortunes are removed
from the impartial and august administration
of the Crown and abandoned to the fierce self-
interest of a small white population. Such
an event is no doubt very remote. Yet the
speculator, the planter, and the settler are
knocking at the door. There are many things
which ought to be done—good, wise, scientific,
and justly profitable. If the Government
cannot find the money to develop the natural
economic strength of the country, to make its
communications, to start its industries, can it
with any reason bar the field to private enterprise? Can it prevent the ingress of a white
population? Ought it to do so, and for how
long? What is to happen when there are
thirty thousand white people in East Africa,
instead of the three thousand or so who make
so much stir at the present time? Perhaps
the course of these chapters will lead us back

again to these questions. I am very doubtful whether it will supply their answers.

We have a discussion in the evening on a much more manageable subject. The District Commissioner at Embo has been ordered by the High Court of the Protectorate to retry a criminal case which he had settled some months before, on account of an informality in the report of the proceedings, which had excited the attention of the revising authority. It is pointed out that neither the accused nor his fellow-natives understand, or can ever be made to understand, the meaning of this repetition of a trial; that they are bewildered; that their confidence in their personal ruler may be weakened; that endless practical difficulties—for instance, the collection of witnesses scattered about in distant villages, and the disquietude caused to them by a second summons from the strange, mysterious power called " Government "—arise out of an error which only a lawyer could detect, and which only appears upon a piece of paper. " Some one," quaintly says a young civil officer, who has ridden over with us, " forgot to say ' Bo !' in the right place." I ask the nature of the " Bo !" It is certainly substantial. No mention was made in the report of the trial that the accused was given the opportunity of cross-examining the hostile witnesses. Therefore, although this was in fact done, the trial is held to be no trial, and ordered anew.

Now, here is again a balancing of disadvantages; but without here examining whether a simple release would not have been better than a retrial, I find myself plainly on the side of the "Bo!" There is scarcely anything more important in the government of men than the exact—I will even say the pedantic—observance of the regular forms by which the guilt or innocence of accused persons is determined. Those forms are designed to protect the prisoner, not merely from the consequences of honest forgetfulness in his judges, but from systematic carelessness and possible oppression. Once they are allowed to be loosely construed the whole system of civilized jurisprudence begins to crumble, and in its place there is gradually erected a rough-and-ready practice dependent entirely for its efficiency and fairness upon the character and intelligence of the individual responsible. Necessary as it is to trust to personal authority in the control of native races of the lowest standard, it is not

less necessary to assign well-marked limits to
that authority, and, above all, to place the
simple primary rights of accused persons to
what we at home are accustomed to call a " fair
trial " outside its scope.   Nor does the admin-
istrator really suffer in native eyes from the
apparition into his domain of superior authority.
The tribesmen see that their ruler—to them
all-powerful, the man of soldiers and police,
of punishment and reward—is himself obedient
to some remote external force, and they wonder
what that mysterious force can be and marvel
dimly at its greatness.   Authority is enhanced
and not impaired by the suggestion of immense
reserves behind and above the immediate ruler
—strong though he be.   But upon this, as
upon other matters, it is not necessary for
every one to be of the same opinion ; and even
lawyers are not always wise.

On our homeward ride in the early morning
we passed a Swahili village.   These Moham-
medans have penetrated deeply and established
themselves widely in the Eastern parts of
Africa.   Armed with a superior religion and
strengthened with Arab blood, they maintain
themselves without difficulty at a far higher
level than the pagan aboriginals among whom

they live.   Their language has become a sort of *lingua franca* over all this part of the world. As traders they are welcomed, as fighting men they are respected, and as sorcerers they are feared by all the tribes.   Their Khan had supplied us with bananas on the previous day with many expressions of apology that, as we were unexpected, he had no " European food." To-day all this was repaired.   The men of the village, to the number of perhaps fifty, walked sedately out to meet us, their long white smocks in striking contrast to the naked, painted barbarians who surrounded them.   The Khan led up a white Arab stallion, of vicious temper and tripling gait, to replace my wearied pony ; and then produced tea and a familiar tin of mixed biscuits, which he had over-night sent runners to procure, that his hospitality might incur no reproach.

While we were eating and parleying with the Khan there arrived on the scene a mounted Kikuyu chief, with chair, umbrella, khaki helmet, and other insignia, and attended by about a hundred warriors in full feather.   In order to show their respect they began at once their war-dance, and we left them a quarter of an hour later still circling and hopping to and

fro with quivering spears and nodding plumes
to their monotonous chorus, while the white-
robed Swahilis stood gravely by and bade us
farewell in the dignified manners of the East.
I reflected upon the interval that separates
these two races from each other, and on the
centuries of struggle that the advance had
cost, and I wondered whether that interval
was wider and deeper than that which divides
the modern European from them both; but
without arriving at any sure conclusion.

Our journey to Embo had been so delightful
that I was not inclined to hanker after rejected
alternatives. But when we drove in to the
Thika camp as the sun was setting, tired out by
fifty miles of road, the first spectacle which
saluted my eyes was a lion's skin spread out
upon the ground and Colonel Wilson engaged in
sprinkling it with arsenical powder. Then we
were told the tale, which in brief was that they
were driving a long reed-bed, when the lion
sprang out and ran obliquely across the line of
beaters. Wilson fired and the lion bounded back
into the reeds, whence stones, fires, shoutings,
shots, and all other disturbances failed to move
him. Whereupon, after two hours, being im-
patient and venturesome, they had marched in

upon him shoulder to shoulder, to find him, fortunately, quite dead.

My friends endeavoured to console me by the news that lions had now been heard of in two other places, and that we should be sure to find one in the morning; and next day, after we had driven three miles of reeds, it seemed that their hopes were well founded, for a large animal of some kind could be seen moving swiftly to and fro under cover, and every one declared this must be the lion. At last only one more patch of reeds remained to beat, and we took up our positions, finger on trigger, about sixty yards from the farther edge of it, while the beaters, raising an astonishing tumult with yells and the beating of tin cans, plunged boldly in. *Parturiunt montes* —out rushed two enormous wart-hogs. Let no one reproach the courage of the pig. These great fierce boars, driven from their last shelter, charged out in gallant style—tusks gleaming, tails perpendicular—and met a fate prepared for a king. With these and another which we galloped down and pistolled on the way home I had to be content, and can now, so far as I am concerned, sadly write, in the expressive words of Reuter, " No lions were ' bagged.' "

CHAPTER III

THE HIGHLANDS OF EAST AFRICA

" Colour " is already the dominant question at Nairobi. " We mean to make East Africa a white man's country," cries, in strident tones, the Colonists' Association on every occasion. Truly a respectable and impressive policy ; but one which seems, at first sight, rather difficult to achieve in a land where there are, so far, fewer than two thousand five hundred whites and more than four million black aboriginals. Can East Africa ever become a white man's country ? Can even the Highlands, with their cool and buoyant breezes and temperate, unchanging climate, become a white man's country ? Never, certainly, in the sense that Canada, or, indeed, the United Kingdom, are white men's countries—that is to say, countries inhabited wholly by white people and sub-sisting upon an economic basis of white un-skilled labour.

It is scarcely worth while even to imagine
the Highlands of East Africa denuded of
their native inhabitants and occupied solely
by Europeans.   Such an idea is utterly impossible.   Whatever may be the increase in
the white population in the future, it is safe
to say that it will be far more than counter-
balanced by the multiplication of the natives,
as they are guarded against famine and prevented from civil war.   But were such a
solution possible, it would be almost the last
thing in the world desired by those who
clamour for " a white man's country."   For
observe it is not against the black aboriginal
that the prejudices and interests of the white
settler or trader are arrayed.   The African, it
is conceded, is welcome to stay in his own
country.   No economic competition has yet
arisen or is likely to arise between him and
the new-comers.   Their spheres of activity lie
wholly apart, for the white man absolutely
refuses to do black man's work ; not for that
harsh toil does he exile himself from the land
of his birth ; while the native could not, in
his present state of development, displace
the white man in skilled employments and
the superintendence and the organization of

industry—even if he would—and nothing is farther from his ambitions.

It is the brown man who is the rival. The European has neither the wish nor the power to constitute a white proletariat in countries like East Africa. In his view the blacks should be the private soldiers of the army, but the non-commissioned officers and the commanders must be white. This should not be dismissed as a mere assertion of racial arrogance. It is an obstinate fact. It is already a grave defect for a community to found itself upon the manual labour of an inferior race, and many are the complications and perils that spring therefrom. But what of the second storey? If there is to be any kind of white society dwelling together year after year within the standards of life and comfort to which Europeans have universally been accustomed to aspire, and largely to attain, this middle stage in the economic system must provide that white society with the means of earning—as professional men, as planters, merchants, traders, farmers, bankers, overseers, contractors, builders, engineers, accountants, clerks—a living for themselves and their families. And here strikes in the

Asiatic. In every single employment of this class, his power of subsisting upon a few shillings a month, his industry, his thrift, his sharp business aptitudes give him the economic superiority, and if economic superiority is to be the final rule—as it has never been and never will be in the history of the world—there is not a single employment of this middle class, from which he will not, to a very large extent, clear the white man, as surely and as remorselessly as the brown rat extirpated the black from British soil.

Then what remains? What sort of social organizations shall we be building up with so much thought and labour in these new lands under the British Crown? There is already no white working class. There is to be no white middle class. Room is left only for the capitalist *pure and simple*—if one may so describe him. A vast army of African labourers, officered by educated Indians or Chinese, and directed by a few individuals of diverse nationalities employing cosmopolitan capital—that is the nightmare which haunts the white population of South Africa, and at which what there is of a white population in East Africa is already shrieking vigorously.

Yet hear the other side. How stands the claim of the British Indian ? His rights as a human being, his rights as a British subject, are equally engaged. It was the Sikh soldier who bore an honourable part in the conquest and pacification of these East African countries. It is the Indian trader who, penetrating and maintaining himself in all sorts of places to which no white man would go or in which no white man could earn a living, has more than any one else developed the early beginnings of trade and opened up the first slender means of communication. It was by Indian labour that the one vital railway on which everything else depends was constructed. It is the Indian banker who supplies perhaps the larger part of the capital yet available for business and enterprise, and to whom the white settlers have not hesitated to recur for financial aid. The Indian was here long before the first British official. He may point to as many generations of useful industry on the coast and inland as the white settlers—especially the most recently-arrived contingents from South Africa (the loudest against him of all)—can count years of residence. Is it possible for any Government with a scrap of respect for honest dealing

4

between man and man, to embark upon a policy of deliberately squeezing out the native of India from regions in which he has established himself under every security of public faith ? Most of all must we ask, is such a policy possible to the Government which bears sway over three hundred millions of our Indian Empire ?

We are in presence of one of those apparently hopeless antagonisms of interests which baffle and dispirit all who are concerned in their adjustment. And these questions are not confined to East Africa or to South Africa. A whole series of new problems has arisen, and will grow graver and larger as the immediate history of the British Empire unfolds. They erect themselves upon a field almost wholly unstudied, and familiar only by the prejudices which in every direction obstruct movement and view. The entry of the Asiatic as labourer, trader, and capitalist into competition in industry and enterprise not only *with*, but *in*, the Western world is a new fact of first importance. Cheap, swift, easy means of communication, the establishment of peace and order over land and sea, the ever-growing inter-dependence of all men and all countries upon one another, have given wings to Asiatic commercial ambition and rendered Asiatic manual labour fluid, as it has never before been fluid since the beginning of things.

Unless these new elements in the economic life of mankind can be scientifically and harmoniously controlled and assimilated, great and novel dangers menace alike the Asiatic and the European he supplants. On the one hand we see the possible exploitation under various unhealthy conditions of immense masses of Asiatic labour, to the moral injury of the employer and to the degradation and suffering of the employed; on the other the overturn of the standards of living laboriously achieved or long obstinately battled for among Europeans. Superadded to these we must foresee the confusion of blood, of manners, of morals, amounting, where operative upon any extensive scale, almost to the disintegration of the existing order of society. And behind— very close behind—lie the appeals to force, by mobs or Empires, to decide in a brutal fashion the brutal question which of two sets of irreconcilable interests shall prevail. It is not easy to measure the degree of political instability that will be introduced into international relations, when the subjects of a powerful military and naval State are continually exposed to penal legislation and open violence, and into private life when the white artisan is invited to acquiesce in his own extinction, in virtue of laws which he himself controls, by a competitor whom, he believes, he could strike down with his hands.

Yet the Asiatic, and here I also include the African native, has immense services to render and energies to contribute to the happiness and material progress of the world. There are spacious lands whose promise can never be realized, there are unnumbered harvests which can never be garnered, without his active co-operation. There are roads and railways and reservoirs which only he can make. There are mines and forests which will slumber for ever without his aid. The mighty continent of tropical Africa lies open to the colonizing and organizing capacities of the East. All those new products which modern industry insistently demands are offered in measureless abundance to the West—if only we could solve the Sphinx's riddle in its newest form.

And is it after all beyond our reach to

provide, if not a perfect, at any rate a practical answer ? There ought to be no insuperable difficulty, in the present state of political knowledge and social organization, in assigning different spheres to the external activity of different races. The Great Powers have partitioned Africa territorially ; is it beyond the wit of man to divide it economically ? The co-operation of many different kinds of men is needed for the cultivation of such a noble estate. Is it impossible to regulate in full and intricate detail the conditions under which that co-operation shall take place ? Here white men can live and thrive ; there they cannot. Here is a task for one, there the opportunity of another. The world is big enough. [I write as the stream of the Nile bears me between the immense spaces of beautiful, fertile, unpopulated country that lie north of the Albert Lake.] There is plenty of room for all. Why cannot we settle it fairly ?

It must be noted that the question of Asiatic immigration presents itself to the Imperial point of view in several quite distinct forms. There are, first of all, colonies which stand on the basis of a white proletariat, and whose inhabitants, rich and poor, employers and employed, are all Europeans. The right of such colonies to forbid the entry of large numbers of Asiatics, and to preserve themselves from the racial chaos and economic disturbance inseparable from such immigration, cannot be denied, although its exercise ought no doubt to be governed by various prudential and other considerations. But these colonies differ markedly from those where the mass of the population is not white, but black, Again, there are colonies which possess responsible government, and where the number of the white middle-class inhabitants very largely exceeds the Asiatic community. It is evident that these stand in a wholly different position from that of places like the tropical Protectorates of East and West Africa.

Indeed, it may be contended that the very fact that the native of British India will undoubtedly, wisely or unwisely, rightly or wrongly, be refused access in any large numbers to several South African and all Australian Colonies by their respective Governments, makes it all the more desirable that the Imperial Government should afford in the tropical Protectorates outlet and scope to the enterprise and colonizing capacity of Hindustan.

And, as I have written, these countries are big enough for all. There is no reason why those Highland areas which promise the white man a home and a career, and where alone he can live in comfort, should not, as a matter of practical administration, be in the main reserved for him. Nor, on the other hand, why the Asiatic, if only he does not teach the African natives evil ways—a contingency which must not be forgotten—should not be encouraged to trade and settle as he will in the enormous regions of tropical fertility to which he is naturally adapted. Somewhere in this direc- tion — I do not wish to dogmatize — the immediate course of sound policy would seem to lie, and, guided by the lights of science and tolerance, we may easily find it.

But the course of these reflections has carried me a good deal farther than the politics of Nairobi would seem to justify ; and I hasten to return to the question with which I started : " Can the Highlands of East Africa be made 'a white man's country' ? " Let us examine this by a fresh process. As one rides or marches through the valleys and across the wide plateaux of these uplands, braced by their delicious air, listening to the music of their streams, and feasting the eye upon their natural wealth and beauty, a sense of bewilderment overcomes the mind.   How is it they have never become the home of some superior race, prosperous, healthy, and free ?   Why is it that, now a railway has opened the door and so much has been published about them, there has not been one furious river of immigration from the cramped and insanitary jungle-slums of Europe ?   Why, most of all, are those who have come—the pioneers, the men of energy and adventure, of large ambitions and strong hands—why are they in so many cases only just keeping their heads above water ?   Why should complaint and discontent and positive discouragement be so general among this limited class ?

I have always experienced a feeling of devout thankfulness never to have possessed a square yard of that perverse commodity called " land." But I will confess that, travelling in the East African Highlands for the first time in my life, I have learned what the sensation of land-hunger is like.   We may repress, but we cannot escape, the desire to peg out one of these fair and wide estates, with all the rewards they offer to industry and inventiveness in the open air.   Yet all around are men possessing thousands of fertile acres, with mountains and rivers and shady trees, acquired for little or nothing, all struggling, all fretful, nervous, high-strung, many disappointed, some despairing, some smashed.

What are the true lineaments concealed behind the veil of boundless promise in which this land is shrouded ? Are they not stamped with mockery ? Is not the eye that regards you fierce as well as bright ? "When I first saw this country," said a colonist to me, "I fell in love with it. I had seen all the best of Australia. I had prospered in New Zealand. I knew South Africa. I thought at last I had struck 'God's own country.' I wrote letters to all my friends urging them to come. I wrote a series of articles in the newspapers praising the splendours of its scenery and the excellence of its climate. Before the last of the articles appeared my capital was nearly expended, my fences had been trampled down by troops of zebra, my imported stock had perished, my title-deeds were still blocked in the Land Office, and I myself had nearly died of a malignant fever. Since then I have left others to extol the glories of East Africa."

These second thoughts err, no doubt, as much on the side of extravagant depression as the first impression was over-sanguine. But that there is a rude reverse to the East African medal is a fact which cannot be disputed, and which ought not, in the interests either of the immigrant or of the country to be concealed. It is still quite unproved that a European can make even the Highlands of East Africa his permanent home—that is to say, that he can live there without sensible degeneration for fifteen or twenty years at a stretch without ever returning to the temperate zones; still less that he can breed and rear families through several generations. The exhilaration of the air must not lead people to forget that an altitude of from five to eight thousand feet above the sea-level is an unusual condition, producing results, not yet ascertained, upon the nervous system, the brain, and the heart. Its coolness can never remove the fact that we are upon the Equator. Although the skies look so familiar and kindly with their white fleecy clouds and passing showers, the direct ray of the sun—almost vertical at all seasons of the year—strikes down on man and beast alike, and woe to the white man whom he finds

uncovered! Although sheep and oxen multiply
so rapidly, although crossing them with imported stock produces in each generation
astonishing improvements in quality, they are
subject to many perils little understood and
often fatal. And if the landscape recalls to
the pensive traveller the peaceful beauties of
gentler climes at home, let him remember
that it nurses with blithe fecundity poisonous
reptiles, and pest-spreading insects, and terrible
beasts of prey.

There is no reason, however, for doubting
that modern science possesses, or will discover, the means of eradicating or mitigating
many of these evils. As the development of
the country and the scientific investigation
of tropical agriculture and tropical disease
proceed, the difficulties which beset the early
settler will gradually be removed. He will
learn how to clothe and house himself; what
to plant, what to breed, and what to avoid.
The spread of East Coast fever, now carried
by the ticks from one animal to another, and
carried by the infected animals from one
district to another, will be arrested, and
controlled by a proper system of wire-fencing
and quarantine. Remedies will be discovered

against the various diseases which attack sheep or horses. Zebra, rhinoceros, buffalo, and other picturesque and fascinating nuisances will be driven from or exterminated within the settled areas, and confined to the ample reserves of uninhabited land. The slow but steady growth of a white population will create a market for local agricultural produce. The powerfully equipped Scientific Departments, the Veterinary and Forestry Departments, and the Department of Agriculture newly established on a considerable scale, will be able to guide and assist the enterprise of the new-comer, and save him from repeating the ill-starred experiments of the pioneer. Roads will improve, and railways and mono-rail tramways will extend. Step by step life and the means of living will become easier and more secure. Still it will not be proved that the pure-bred European can rear his children under the Equatorial sun and at an elevation of more than six thousand feet; and till that is proved " the white man's country " will remain a white man's dream.

I have written of Europeans and Asiatics. What of the African? About four millions of these dark folk are comprised within the districts of the East Africa Protectorate which are actually or partially administered. Many more lie beyond those wide and advancing boundaries. What is to be their part in shaping the future of their country? It is, after all, *their* Africa. What are they going to do for it, and what is it going to do for them? "The natives," says the planter, "evince a great reluctance to work, especially to work regularly." "They must be made to work," say others. "Made to work for whom?" we innocently ask. "For us, of course," is the ready answer; "what did you think we meant?" And here we run into another herd of rhinoceros questions—awkward, thick-skinned, and horned, with a short sight, an evil temper, and a tendency to rush blindly up wind upon any alarm. Is the native idle? Does he not keep himself and pay his taxes? Or does he loll at his ease while his three or four wives till the soil, bear the burden, and earn his living? And if idle, has he a right to remain idle—a naked and unconscious philosopher, living "the simple life," without cares or wants, — a gentleman of leisure in a panting world? Is that to be the last word? Is civilization to say definitely that when the African native has kept himself, or made his women keep him, she has no further claim upon him? The white man shall do the rest. He shall preserve the peace, that the tribes may prosper and multiply. His watchful and fore-seeing eye, strained and weary with the effort, shall still make provision against famine; his science, though he himself goes down in the struggle, shall grapple with pestilence and cure disease. Far from his home or from his family he shall hew the trees and dig the wells, shall dam the streams and build the roads, with anxious heart and "in the sweat of his brow," according to the curse laid upon the child of many wants, while the child of few wants watches him from the shade and thinks him mad.

And to compare the life and lot of the African aboriginal—secure in his abyss of con-tented degradation, rich in that he lacks every-thing and wants nothing—with the long night-mare of worry and privation, of dirt and gloom and squalour, lit only by gleams of torturing knowledge and tantalizing hope, which consti tutes the lives of so many poor people in England and Scotland, is to feel the ground tremble under foot. "It would never do to have a lot of 'mean whites' in this country," I heard one day a gentleman say. "It would destroy the respect of the native for the white man, if he saw what miserable people we have got at home." So here, at any rate, the boot is on the other leg, and Civilization is ashamed of her arrangements in the presence of a savage, embarrassed lest he should see what lies behind the gold and purple robe of State, and begin to suspect that the all-powerful white man is a fraud. But this is an irrelevancy!

I am clearly of opinion that no man has a right to be idle, whoever he be or wherever he lives. He is bound to go forward and take an honest share in the general work of the world. And I do not except the African native. To a very much larger extent than is often recognized by some who discuss these questions, the natives are industrious, willing to learn, and capable of being led forward. Live for a few weeks, as I have done, in close association with the disciplined soldiers of the King's African Rifles, or with the smart sailors of the Uganda Marine, and it seems

wonderful to contrast them with the population from which they have emerged. How
strong, how good-natured, how clever they
are! How proud their white officers are
of them! What pains they take to please
the travellers whom they escort; how frankly
they are delighted by a word of praise or
thanks! Just and honourable discipline, careful education, sympathetic comprehension,
are all that is needed to bring a very large
proportion of the native tribes of East Africa
to a far higher social level than that at
which they now stand. And why should
men only be taught to be soldiers? Is war
always to have the best of everything? Cannot peaceful industry be made as attractive,
be as highly organized, as carefully studied
as the combined use of deadly weapons?
"Why," as Ruskin asks, "cannot men take
pride in *building* villages instead of only
carrying them?"

I wonder why my pen slips off into these
labyrinths, when all I set out to do was to
give some general idea of politics at Nairobi?
But in truth the problems of East Africa are
the problems of the world. We see the
social, racial, and economic stresses which

rack modern society already at work here, but in miniature ; and if we choose to study the model when the whole engine is at hand, it is because on the smaller scale we can see more clearly, and because in East Africa and Uganda the future is still uncompromised. The British Government has it in its hands to shape the development and destiny of these new countries and their varied peoples with an authority and from an elevation far superior to that with which Cabinets can cope with the giant tangles at home. And the fact stirs the mind. But by this time the reader will have had as much of East African politics as I had when, after three days of deputations and disputations, the train steamed out of Nairobi to take us to the Great Lake and beyond.

CHAPTER IV

THE GREAT LAKE

WE are off again on the Uganda Railway. Interesting and beautiful as is the country through which the line passes from Mombasa to Nairobi, it is surpassed by the magnificent scenery of the journey to the Lake. First in order and in rank is the Great Rift. This curious fault in the earth's surface, which geologists trace across the four thousand miles of land and sea which separate us from Palestine, and onward still to the southern end of Lake Tanganyika, is traversed by the Uganda Railway at one of its most remarkable stages. For sixty miles the Highland plateau has been rising steadily by a succession of wooded undulations to a level of over six thousand feet. Now it falls abruptly, almost precipitously, more than two thousand feet. This frowning wall of rock and forest, which extends straight as a ruler farther than eye

66

THE RIFT VALLEY FROM THE KIKUYU ESCARPMENT.

P. 66.

can see, is the Kikuyu Escarpment. As the train claws its way downwards by slant and zigzag along its face, a majestic panorama breaks upon the view. Far below, bathed in sunshine, stretching away to misty purple horizons, lie the broad expanses of the Rift Valley. Its level surface is broken by strangely moulded volcanic hills and shattered craters. The opposite mountain wall looms up in the far distance, brown and blue. We gaze down upon the plain as from a balloon, mistaking forests for patches of green grass, and mighty trees for thorn-scrub.

Another hour or so and Lake Naivasha comes into view. This sheet of water is about ten miles square, and the rim of a submerged crater makes an odd, crescent-shaped island in its midst. Its brackish waters repel the inhabitants, but afford shelter to numberless wild-fowl and many hippopotami. At Naivasha there is the Government stock farm. One may see in their various flocks the native sheep, the half-bred English, the three-quarter-bred, etc. The improvement is amazing. The native sheep is a hairy animal, looking to the unpractised eye more like a goat than a sheep. Crossed with Sussex or Australian blood, his descendant is transformed into a woolled beast of familiar aspect. At the next cross the progeny is almost indistinguishable from the pure-bred English in appearance, but better adapted to the African sun and climate. It is the same with cattle. In the first generation the hump of the African ox vanishes. In the second he emerges a respectable British Shorthorn. The object of this farm is twofold: first, to find the type best adapted to local conditions; secondly, to supply the settlers and the natives with a steadily broadening fountain of good blood by which their flocks and herds may be trebled and quadrupled in value. The enthusiasm and zeal of those in charge of this work were refreshing. ' At present, however, their operations are restricted by insufficient funds and by the precautions which must be taken against East Coast fever. The first of these impediments may be removed ; the second is less tractable.

East Coast fever came across the German border a year and a half ago, and since then, in spite of such preventive measures as our scanty means allow, it has been gradually and slowly spreading through the Protectorate. A diseased cow may take thirty days to die.

GOVERNMENT FARM AT NAIVASHA.

P 68.

In the meantime wherever it goes the swarming ticks are infected. They hold their poison for a year. If, during that time, other cattle pass over the ground the ticks fasten upon them and inoculate them with the sickness. And each new victim wanders off to spread the curse to new ticks, who cast it back to new cattle, and so on till the end of the story. At each point fresh areas of ground become distempered, and fresh cows begin to drop off one by one, leaving their evil inheritance to the ravening insects.

So here we see the two principles of Nature at work simultaneously—the blood-stock rams and bulls spreading their healthy, fruitful life in ever-widening circles through the land; the infected cattle carrying their message of death in all directions. Every point that either attains, becomes at once a new centre of vitality or dissolution. Both processes march deliberately forward to limitless multiplications. The native is helpless in the face of advancing ruin. Left to itself the evil would assuredly devour the good, till the cattle were exterminated and the sickness starved to death for lack of prey. But at this moment the white biped with faculties of ratiocination intervenes from the tin-roofed Department of Agriculture; discovers, for instance, that ground may be purified by putting upon it sheep, into whom the ticks discharge their poison harmlessly and are thereafter purged; erects hundreds of miles of wire fencing to cut the country up into compartments, as a warship is divided by bulkheads; encloses infected areas; destroys suspected animals; searches methodically and ever more hopefully for prophylactics and remedies; with one hand arrests the curse, with the other speeds the blessing, and in so doing is surely discharging rather an important function from a good many points of view.

My friends and I took four days in travelling to the Victoria Nyanza, although the distance can be covered in twenty-four hours; for we turned aside every day for sport or business, while our train waited obligingly in a siding. Of the latter, indeed, there was no lack, for the Governor and the heads of several departments were in the train, and we laboured faithfully together at many prickly things. Then at the stations came farmers, surveyors, and others, with words of welcome or complaint, and a deputation of Boer settlers with

THE LAIBON'S WIVES.

RAILHEAD AT KISUMU.   P. 71.

many expressions of loyalty to the Crown, and the chiefs of the Lumbwa and Nandi tribes, with a crowd of warriors, and their Laibon with his four wives, all in a row, till I was as tired of making "brief and appropriate" speeches as my companions must have been of hearing them.

But Elmenteita was all holiday. Lord Delamere met us at the station with Cape carts, ponies, and hog-spears, and we drove off in search of pig over an enormous plain thickly peopled with antelope and gazelle. I cannot pretend to the experience of both countries necessary to compare the merits of pig-sticking in India and in East Africa in respect of the fighting qualities of the animal, nor the ground over which he is pursued. But I should think the most accomplished member of the Meerut Tent Club would admit that the courage and ferocity of the African wart-hog, and the extreme roughness of the country, heaped as it is with boulders and pitted with deep ant-bear holes concealed by high grass, make pig-sticking in East Africa a sport which would well deserve his serious and appreciative attention. At present it is in its infancy, and very few even of the officers of the King's African

Rifles can boast the proficiency of the Indian expert. But everything in East Africa is at its first page; and besides, the wart-hog is, at present at any rate, regarded as dangerous vermin who does incredible damage to native plantations, and whose destruction—by any method, even the most difficult—is useful as well as exciting.

Our first pig was a fine fellow, who galloped off with his tail straight up in the air and his tusks gleaming mischievously, and afforded a run of nearly three miles before he was killed. The risk of the sport consists in this—that the pig cannot be overtaken and effectively speared except by a horse absolutely at full gallop. The ground is so trappy that one hardly cares to take one's eyes off it for a moment. Yet during at least a hundred yards at a time the whole attention of the rider must be riveted on the pig, within a few yards of whom he is riding, and who may be expected to charge at any second. A fall at such a climax is necessarily very dangerous, as the wart-hog would certainly attack the unhorsed cavalier; yet no one can avoid the chance. I do not know whether Anglo-India will shudder, but I should certainly recommend the intending hunter in

East Africa to strap a revolver on his thigh in case of accidents. "You do not want it often," as the American observed; "but when you do, you want it badly."

We passed a jolly morning riding after these brutes and shooting a few *Gazella Granti* and *Gazella Thomsoni*, or "Grants" and "Tommies" as they are familiarly called, and in looking for eland in the intervals. At the end of Lake Elmenteita, a beautiful sheet of water, unhappily brackish, a feast had been prepared, to which a number of gentlemen from Lord Delamere's estates and the surrounding farms had been bidden. A long array of flocks and herds was marshalled on both sides of the track in due order, native-bred, half-bred, three-quarter-bred, pure. Through these insignia of patriarchal wealth, which would have excited the keenest interest in any traveller less hungry and more instructed in such matters than I, we made our way to an excellent luncheon, which, be sure, was not unaccompanied by the usual discussion on East African politics.

It was late in the afternoon when we started back to the train, which lay eight miles off in a siding. On the way we fell in with a most fierce and monstrous pig, who led us a nice dance through bush and grass and boulder. As he emerged into a patch of comparatively smooth, open ground I made up my mind to spear him, urged my pony to her top speed, and was just considering how best to do the deed when, without the slightest provocation, or, at any rate, before he had been even pricked, the pig turned sharp round and sprang at me, as if he were a leopard. Luckily, my spear got in the way, and with a solid jar, which made my arm stiff for a week, drove deep into his head and neck before it broke, so that he was glad to sheer off with eighteen inches of it sticking in him, and after a dash at my companion he took refuge in a deep hole, from which no inducements or insults could draw him.

Later we rode and killed another pig and chased a fourth unsuccessfully, and it was nearly dark before the railway was reached. As I was getting into my carriage they calmly told me that *six lions* had walked across the line a quarter of a mile away and a quarter of an hour before. A settler who had been to lunch at Elmenteita was loading a hastily-borrowed revolver before starting on his homeward ride to Nakuru, and as I gave him some cartridges, I reflected that, whatever may be the shortcomings of East Africa, the absence of an interesting and varied fauna is certainly not among them.

Next day our train is climbing through dense and beautiful forests to the summit of the Mau Escarpment. Admiration of the wealth and splendour of the leafy kingdom is mingled with something very like awe at its aggressive fertility. The great trees overhang the line. The creepers trail down the cuttings, robing the red soil with cloaks of flowers and foliage. The embankments are already covered. Every clearing is densely overgrown with sinuous plants. But for the ceaseless care with which the whole line is scraped and weeded it would soon become impassable. As it is, the long fingers of the encroaching forest are every-where stretching out enviously towards the bright metals. Neglect the Uganda Railway for a year, and it would take an expedition to discover where it had run.

At Nyoro station nearly nine hundred natives were at work cutting timber for the railway, which is entirely dependent on wood fuel. The contractor in charge, a young

English gentleman, who was described to me as being a model employer of native labour in Government contracts, had taken the trouble to cut a path through the forest across a loop of the line in order that I might see what it was like inside. Through this leafy tunnel, about a mile and a half long, we all accordingly dived. There was nothing sinister in the aspect of this forest, for all its density and confusion. The great giants towered up magnificently to a hundred and fifty feet. Then came the ordinary forest trees, much more thickly clustered. Below this again was a layer of scrub and bushes ; and under, around, and among the whole flowed a vast sea of convolvulus-looking creeper. Through all this four-fold veil the sunlight struggled down every twenty yards or so in gleaming chequers of green and gold.

On the way the method of fuel-cutting is explained. So far as the labourer is concerned, it is an elaborate system of piece-work, very accurately and fairly adjusted, and, as is so often the case where the white employer takes personal care of his men, there appeared to be no difficulty in finding any number of natives. But they are a plaguey company. Few will

stay for more than a month or two, however
satisfied they may be with their work and
its rewards; and just as they begin to get
skilful, off they go to their villages to cultivate
their gardens and their families, promising to
come back another year, or after the harvest,
or at some other remote and indefinite date.
And meanwhile the railway must have its
fuel every day and day after day, with
the remorseless monotony of the industrial
machine.

But what a way to cut fuel! A floating
population of clumsy barbarians pecking at
the, trees with native choppers more like a
toy hoe than an axe, and carrying their loads
when completed a quarter of a mile on their
heads to the wood-stack, while the forest
laughs at the feebleness of man. I made a
calculation. Each of the nine hundred natives
employed costs on the whole six pounds a
year. The price of a steam tree-felling plant,
with a mile of mono-rail tram complete, is
about five hundred pounds. The interest and
sinking fund on this capital outlay represent
the wages of four natives, to which must
be added the salary of a competent white
engineer, equal to the wage of forty natives,

and the working expenses and depreciation roughly estimated at the wage of twenty natives more; in all the wage of sixty-five natives. Such a plant, able to cut trees six feet in diameter through in four or five minutes, to cut timber as well as fuel, to saw it into the proper lengths for every purpose with the utmost rapidity, and to transport it by whole truck-loads when sawn to the railway siding, would accomplish a week's work of the sixty-five natives it replaced in a single day, and effect a sevenfold multiplication of power. It is no good trying to lay hold of Tropical Africa with naked fingers. Civilization must be armed with machinery if she is to subdue these wild regions to her authority. Iron roads, not jogging porters; tireless engines, not weary men; cheap power, not cheap labour; steam and skill, not sweat and fumbling: there lies the only way to tame the jungle—more jungles than one.

On this we talked—or at least I talked—while we scrambled across the stumps of fallen trees or waded in an emerald twilight from one sunbeam to another across the creeper flood. It is of vital importance that these forests should not be laid waste by reckless and improvident hands. It is not less important that the Uganda Railway should have cheap fuel. For a long time fuel alone was the object, but now that an elaborate Forestry Department has been established on the most scientific lines, there is a danger that forestry will be the only object, and the cost of fuel so raised by regulations, admirable in themselves, that the economy of the Uganda Railway may be impaired. And let us never forget that the Uganda Railway is the driving-wheel of the whole concern. What is needed here, as elsewhere, is a harmonious compromise between opposite and conflicting interests. That is all.

Presently our guide began to tell us of the strange creatures who live in the forest, and are sometimes seen quite close by the fuel-cutters—very rare antelope, enormous buffaloes, and astonishing birds and butterflies beyond imagination. He had managed to make friends with the Wandorobo—a tribe of forest-dwelling natives who live plunged in these impenetrable shades, who are so shy that, if once a stranger does but set eye upon their village, forthwith they abandon it; yet who are at the same time so teased by curiosity that they cannot resist peeping, peeping ever nearer and nearer to the fuel-cutters, until one day commercial relations are established on the basis of sugar for skins. I was just becoming interested in these wood-squirrels when we broke into the hot blaze of the noonday sun beating down on the polished railway track, and had to climb up on to our cowcatcher in order to hurry on to a real steam saw-mill ten miles farther up the line.

As the journey advances, the train mounts steadily higher and the aspect of the country changes. The forest, which has hitherto lapped the line closely on every side, now makes fair division with rolling hills of grass. And there is this extraordinary feature about it: where the forest areas end, they end abruptly. There is no ragged belt of trees less thickly grown; no transition. Smooth slopes of grass run up to the very edge of virgin forest, just as in England the meadow runs to the edge of the covert. The effect is to make the landscape surprisingly homelike. It is like travelling through a series of gigantic parks, where the hand of man has for hundreds of years decided exactly where trees shall grow and where they shall not.

KAVIRONDO WARRIORS AT KISUMU.

P. 80

Towards the west great plains are visible, in misty apparition, through rifts in the plateau. At length we arrive at the summit of the escarpment, and stop for luncheon by an indicator, which registers eight thousand two hundred and ninety feet above the sea-level. Southward rises a hill perhaps five hundred feet above us, from the top of which the waters of the Great Lake can be seen, like the waters of a distant ocean.

Geographically we have now reached the culminating point in this long journey. Henceforward, to find our way home, we have only to descend, guided by the force of gravity, first swiftly along the railroad to the Victoria Lake, then sedately with the stream of the Nile to the Mediterranean. The lofty table-lands of East Africa, with their crisp, chill air and English aspect, must now be left behind —not without many regrets—and the traveller will alight upon a middle world spread at a level of about four thousand feet, in which an entirely different order of conditions prevails. Downward then at thirty miles an hour, along the side of spacious valleys, around the shoulders of the hills, across thin-spun iron bridges, through whose girders one glances

6

down at torrents flashing far below, onward to
the Lake.   Within an hour the temperature
has sensibly altered.   An overcoat is no longer
necessary, even if you ride in front of the
engine.   In two hours the climate is warm
and damp with the steamy heat of the Tropics.
The freshness has gone out of the air, and in its
place is that sense of sultry oppression which
precedes the thunderstorms so common at this
season of the year.

In order to avoid a hot night on the Lake
shore we stopped at Fort Ternan, a placeless
name, some forty miles from Kisumu, and
rather more than a thousand feet above it.
And here the storm which had been brooding
all the afternoon over the western face of the
Mau Escarpment burst upon us.   Even after
ten months on the South African veldt I was
astonished by its fury.   For nearly two hours
the thunder crashed and roared in tremendous
peals—

> "Like water flung from some high crag,
>   The lightning fell with never a jag,
>   A river steep and wide,"

while the rain dashed down in sheets of water,
one single gust of which would drench you to
the skin.   But our train is an effective shelter.

We dine comfortably in the midst of the tempest, and afterwards in a cooler atmosphere look up towards repentant stars and a tear-stained sky.

At dawn we are at Kisumu. There is a stir of men, a crowded platform, soldiers in order, groups of Indian traders, hundreds of Kavirondo natives in their fullest undress, bunting, and introductions. Large white steamers lie alongside the jetty, and beyond these the waters of the Lake gleam their broad welcome to the sunrise. Kisumu, or Port Florence as it is sometimes called, is the western terminus of the Uganda Railway and the chief port on Lake Victoria. It possesses what I am told is the highest dockyard in the world, and is the place at which all the steamers now plying on the Lake have been put together. One eight-hundred-ton cargo boat is actually in process of construction, and will be launched in a few months' time to meet the growing traffic of the Nyanza. The station itself is pretty ; its trim houses and shady trees, backed against the hills, overlook the wide expanse of Kavirondo Bay and its encircling promontories. Unluckily, it is unhealthy, for the climate is depressing and the sewage accumulates in the tideless and shallow inlet. Some day one of two things

will happen : either the waters of the Victoria
Nyanza will be raised by a dam across the
Ripon Falls and Kavirondo Bay will be proportionately deepened and cleansed, or the
railway will be deflected and prolonged to its
natural terminus on the deep waters of the lake
at Port Victoria.

The Kavirondo tribe, the greatest in this
part of the country, had organized an imposing
demonstration. In dense array they lined the
road from the station to the Commissioner's
house, and our party walked through their
midst in a perfect hubbub of horns and drums
and shrill salutations. All the warriors carried
their spears, shields, and war-paint, and most of
them wore splendid plumes of ostrich feathers.
The Kavirondo are naked and unashamed.
Both sexes are accustomed to walk about in
the primitive simplicity of Nature. Their
nudity is based not upon mere ignorance but
reasoned policy. They have a very strong
prejudice against the wearing of clothes, which
they declare lead to immorality; and no
Kavirondo woman can attire herself even in
the most exiguous raiment without sullying
her reputation. They are said to be the most
moral of all the tribes dwelling on the Lake
shore. It is a pity that Herr Diogenes

NANDI AND KAVIRONDO WARRIORS AT KISUMU.

P. 84.

Teufelsdröckh, of the University of Weiss-
nichtwo, did not meet them in his rugged
wanderings, for they would surely have enabled
him to add another page to his monumental
work on the functions of the tailor.

I wake up the next morning to find myself
afloat on a magnificent ship. Its long and
spacious decks are as snowy as those of a
pleasure yacht. It is equipped with baths,
electric light, and all modern necessities.
There is an excellent table, also a well-selected
library. Smart bluejackets—with ebon faces
—are polishing the brasswork; dapper, white-
clad British naval officers pace the bridge.
We are steaming ten miles an hour across
an immense sea of fresh water as big as
Scotland, and uplifted higher than the summit
of Ben Nevis. At times we are in a complete
circle of lake and sky, without a sign of land.
At others we skirt lofty coasts covered with
forest and crowned with distant blue-brown
mountains, or thread our course between a
multitude of beautiful islands. The air is cool
and fresh, the scenery splendid. We might be
yachting off the coast of Cornwall in July.
We are upon the Equator, in the heart of
Africa, and crossing the Victoria Nyanza, four
thousand feet above the sea!

CHAPTER V

THE KINGDOM OF UGANDA

THE East Africa Protectorate is a country
of the highest interest to the colonist, the
traveller, or the sportsman. But the Kingdom
of Uganda is a fairy tale. You climb up a
railway instead of a beanstalk, and at the end
there is a wonderful new world. The scenery
is different, the vegetation is different, the
climate is different, and, most of all, the people
are different from anything elsewhere to be
seen in the whole range of Africa. Instead of
the breezy uplands we enter a tropical garden.
In the place of naked, painted savages, clashing
their spears and gibbering in chorus to their
tribal chiefs, a complete and elaborate polity is
presented. Under a dynastic King, with a
Parliament, and a powerful feudal system, an
amiable, clothed, polite, and intelligent race
dwell together in an organized monarchy upon
the rich domain between the Victoria and Albert

KISUMU.

P. 86.

Lakes. More than two hundred thousand natives are able to read and write. More than one hundred thousand have embraced the Christian faith. There is a Court, there are Regents and Ministers and nobles, there is a regular system of native law and tribunals; there is discipline, there is industry, there is culture, there is peace. In fact, I ask myself whether there is any other spot in the whole earth where the dreams and hopes of the negrophile, so often mocked by results and stubborn facts, have ever attained such a happy realization.

Three separate influences, each of them powerful and benevolent, exercise control over the mass of the Baganda nation. First, the Imperial authority, secular, scientific, disinterested, irresistible; secondly, a native Government and feudal aristocracy, corrected of their abuses, yet preserving their vitality; and thirdly, missionary enterprise on an almost unequalled scale. Under the shelter of the British Flag, safe from external menace or internal broil, the child-King grows to a temperate and instructed maturity. Surrounded by his officers of State, he presides at the meetings of his council and Parliament, or worships in the huge thatched cathedral which has been reared on Namirembe Hill. Fortified in their rights, but restrained from tyrannical excess, and guided by an outside power, his feudatories exercise their proper functions. The people, relieved from the severities and confusions of times not long ago, are apt to learn and willing to obey. And among them with patient energy toils a large body of devoted Christian men of different nations, of different Churches, but of a common charity, tending their spiritual needs, enlarging their social and moral conceptions, and advancing their education year by year.

An elegance of manners springing from a naïve simplicity of character pervades all classes. An elaborate ritual of friendly salutations relieves the monotony of the wayfarer's journey. Submission without servility or loss of self-respect is accorded to constituted authority. The natives evince an eagerness to acquire knowledge and a very high observant and imitative faculty. And then Uganda is from end to end one beautiful garden, where the staple food of the people grows almost without labour, and where almost everything else can be grown better and easier than anywhere else. The planter from the best islands in the West Indies is astonished at the richness of the soil. Cotton grows everywhere. Rubber, fibre, hemp, cinnamon, cocoa, coffee, tea, coca, vanilla, oranges, lemons, pineapples are natural or thrive on introduction. As for our English garden products, brought in contact with the surface of Uganda they simply give one wild bound of efflorescence or fruition and break their hearts for joy. Does it not sound a paradise on earth? Approach and consider it more closely.

The good ship *Clement Hill*, named after a well-known African explorer, has carried us smoothly and prosperously across the northern corner of the Victoria Nyanza, and reaches the pier of Entebbe as the afternoon draws towards its close. The first impression that strikes the eye of the visitor fresh from Kavirondo is the spectacle of hundreds of natives all dressed in long clean white garments which they wear with dignity and ease. At the landing-place a sort of pavilion has been erected, and here come deputations from the Chamber of Commerce— a limited body of Europeans—from the Goanese community, and from the numerous Indian colony of merchants. A tonga drawn by two mules takes me to Government House, and from a wide mosquito-proof veranda I am able to survey a truly delightful prospect. The most beautiful plants and trees grow in profusion on all sides. Beyond a blaze of violet, purple, yellow, and crimson blossoms, and an expanse of level green lawns, the great blue lake lies in all its beauty. The hills and islands on the horizon are just beginning to flush to the sunset. The air is soft and cool. Except that the picture actually looks more English in its character, one would imagine it was the Riviera. It must be too good to be true.

It *is* too good to be true. One can hardly believe that such an attractive spot can be cursed with malignant attributes. Yet what is true of the East Africa Protectorate is even more true of Uganda. The contrast between appearance and reality is more striking and more harsh. Behind its glittering mask Entebbe wears a sinister aspect. These smiling islands which adorn and diversify the scenery of the lake supported a few years ago a large population. To-day they are desolate. Every white man seems to feel a sense of undefinable oppression. A cut will not heal; a scratch

GOVERNMENT HOUSE, ENTEBBE.

P. 90

festers. In the third year of residence even a small wound becomes a running sore. One day a man feels perfectly well; the next, for no apparent cause, he is prostrate with malaria, and with malaria of a peculiarly persistent kind, turning often in the third or fourth attack to blackwater fever. In the small European community at Entebbe there have been quite recently two suicides. Whether, as I have suggested in East Africa, it be the altitude, or the downward ray of the Equatorial sun, or the insects, or some more subtle cause, there seems to be a solemn veto placed upon the white man's permanent residence in these beautiful abodes.

There are many who advocate the abandonment of Entebbe as the administrative capital and the restoration of the seat of Government to Kampala. But the expense of transferring public offices and buildings lately erected to another site is altogether beyond the slender resources and not among the most urgent needs of the Uganda Protectorate. Great improvements have been effected recently in the sanitation of Entebbe. The bush and trees, which added so greatly to its picturesque appearance, have been ruthlessly cut down;

and with them, *mirabile dictu,* have vanished
the mosquito and the sleeping-sickness tsetse-
fly.   Half a mile away on either side of the
settlement are groves which it might easily be
death to enter ; but the inhabited area is now
quite clear.

Besides, the general unhealthiness of the
country so far as the European is concerned
is not local to Entebbe.   It is widely spread
in slightly different degrees throughout the
whole of Uganda ; and Kampala is certainly
not exempt.   Finally, there is a reason of a
different character which ought to impose a
final bar on any return of the Imperial Government to the native city.   Uganda is a native
state.   Much of our success in dealing with its
population arises from the fact that we work
through and by the native Government.   And
that Government could not fail to lose much,
if not all, of its separate and natural identity
if it were overwhelmed by the immediate
proximity of the supreme Administration.

For a new station in an almost unknown
land, Entebbe certainly presents many remarkable evidences of progress.   The slopes of the
lake shore are covered with pretty villas, each
standing in its own luxuriant garden.   There

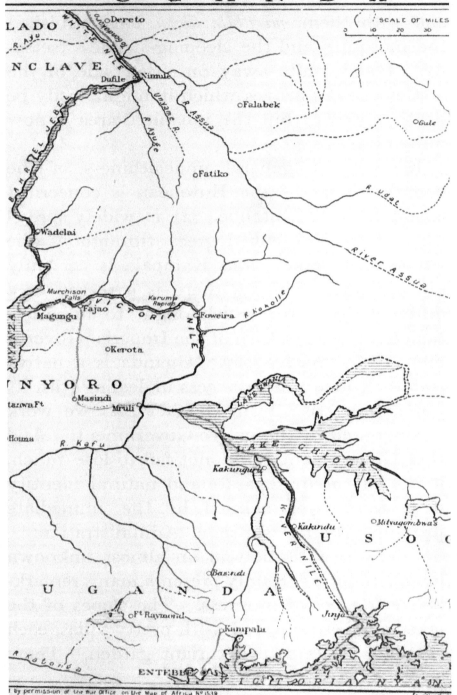

is an excellent golf course, and a very bright and pleasant society. Guardian over all this stands the Sikh. There are two companies of these soldiers, one at Entebbe and the other at Kampala, who, being entirely immune to local influences of all kinds, constitute what Mr. Gladstone used to call the "motor muscle" of Imperial authority. I have always admired the Sikh in India, both in his cantonments and in the field. But somehow his graceful military figure and grave countenance under the turban as he stands erect beside his rifle on guard over British interests six thousand miles from the Punjab, impresses the eye and the imagination with an added force. He is a picked volunteer from all the Sikh regiments, who delights in Uganda, thrives under its, to him, milder sun, lives on nothing, saves his doubled pay, and returns to India enriched and proud of his service across the sea. If at any time considerations of expense, or the desire to obtain a complete homogeneity in the military forces of the Protectorate, should lead to the disbandment or withdrawal of these two companies, those who take the decision will have incurred a responsibility which few would care to share with them.

So far as human force is concerned, the British power in these regions is at present beyond challenge. No man can withstand it. But a new opponent has appeared and will not be denied. Uganda is defended by its insects. It would even seem that the arrival of the white man and the increased movement and activity which his presence has engendered have awakened these formidable atoms to a realization of their powers of evil. The dreaded *Spirillum* tick has begun to infest the roads like a tiny footpad, and scarcely any precautions avail with certainty against him. This tick is a dirty, drab-coloured creature the size and shape of a small squashed pea. When he bites an infected person he does not contract the Spirillum fever himself, nor does he transmit it directly to other persons. By a peculiarly malevolent provision of Nature this power is exercised not by him but by his descendants, who are numbered in hundreds. So the poison spreads in an incalculable progression. Although this fever is not fatal, it is exceptionally painful in its course and distressing in its consequences. There are five or six separate and successive attacks of fever, in which the temperature of the victim may rise even to 107 degrees ; and afterwards the eyes and hearing are temporarily affected by a kind of facial paralysis. Road after road has been declared infected by this scourge, and officer after officer struck down as he moves on duty from place to place. The only sure preventive seems to be the destruction of all old grass-huts and camping-grounds, and the erection along the roads of a regular system of stone-built, properly maintained and disinfected rest-houses, in which the traveller may take refuge from the lurking peril. And this will have to be done.

But a far more terrible shadow darkens the Uganda Protectorate. In July, 1901, a doctor of the Church Missionary Society Hospital at Kampala noticed eight cases of a mysterious disease. Six months later he reported that over two hundred natives had died of it in the Island of Buvuma, and that thousands appeared to be infected. The pestilence swiftly spread through all the districts of the lake shore, and the mortality was appalling. No one could tell where it had come from or what it was caused by. It resisted every kind of treatment and appeared to be universally fatal. Scientific inquiries of various kinds were immediately set on foot, but for a long time no results were obtained, and meanwhile the disease ran along the coasts and islands of the great lake like fire in a high wind. By the middle of 1902 the reported deaths from *Trypanosomiasis,* or " sleeping sickness," as it has come to be called, numbered over thirty thousand.   It was still spreading rapidly upon all sides, and no clue whatever to its treatment or prevention had been obtained.   It seemed certain that the entire population of the districts affected was doomed.

On April 28th, 1903, Colonel Bruce, whose services had been obtained for the investigation of " sleeping sickness " through the instrumentality of the Royal Society, announced that he considered the disease to be due to a kind of trypanosome, conveyed from one person to another by the bite of a species of tsetse-fly called *Glossina palpalis.*   His theory was strongly supported by the fact that the disease appeared to be confined to the localities infested by the fly.   The fly-belt also could be defined with precision, and was rarely found to extend more than a mile or two from water.   The news that Europeans could no longer consider themselves immune from the

infection caused, as might be imagined, much
consternation in the white community. Nearly
everybody had been bitten by tsetses at one
time or another, but whether by this particular
species when actually infected, remained in
suspense. Moreover, tsetse-flies abounded in
such numbers on all parts of the lake shore
that their wholesale destruction seemed quite
impossible. What then?

For a time Colonel Bruce's discovery
almost paralyzed all preventive and restric-
tive measures. The scourge fell unchecked.
By the end of 1903 the reported deaths
numbered over ninety thousand, and the
lake shores were becoming fast depopulated.
Whole villages were completely exterminated,
and great tracts in Usoga, which had formerly
been famed for their high state of cultivation,
relapsed into forests. The weakness of the
victims and the terror or apathy of the sur-
vivors permitted a sudden increase in the
number of leopards, and these fierce animals
preyed with daring and impunity upon the
living, the dying, and the dead.

Further investigations, which were anxiously
pushed on in many directions, revealed the
existence of the tsetse-fly over widespread

7

areas. In the interior of Usoga, on the banks of many rivers, in swamps on the shores of the Albert Lake and Lake Albert Edward, these swarming emissaries of death were found to be awaiting their message. All that was needed to arm them with their fatal power was the arrival of some person infected with the microbe. The Albert shores and several parts of the Upper Nile soon became new centres of pestilence. Thousands of deaths occurred in Unyoro. By the end of 1905 considerably more than two hundred thousand persons had perished in the plague-stricken regions, *out of a population* in those regions *which could not have exceeded three hundred thousand.*|

Any decrease in the mortality in any district up to the present time is due, not to any diminution in the virulence of the disease, but simply to the reduction of possible victims, owing to the extermination of the inhabitants. Buvuma, a few years ago one of the most prosperous of all the islands, contains fewer than fourteen thousand out of thirty thousand. Some of the islands in the Sesse group have lost every soul, while in others a few moribund natives, crawling about in the last stages of the disease, are all that are left to represent a once teeming population.

" It might have been expected," writes Sir H. Hesketh Bell, the Governor of Uganda, to whom I am indebted for much valuable information on this subject, " that, even though the negroes showed inability to grasp the theory of the transmission of disease by the agency of insects, the undeniable deadliness of the countries bordering on the lake shore would have induced them to flee from the stricken land and to have sought in the healthier districts inland a refuge from the pestilence that was slaying them by thousands. An extraordinary fatalism, however, seems to have paralyzed the natives, and, while deploring the sadness of their fate, they appear to have accepted death almost with apathy."

The police of science, although arrived late on the scene of the tragedy, were now following many converging clues. Therapeutic investigation into the treatment and origin of the disease, entomological examination of the resorts, habits, dangers, and life-history of the fly, and thirdly administrative measures of drastic authority are now being driven sternly forward. Knowledge has accumulated.

Fighting the sleeping sickness is like laying
a vampire. To make the spell work, five
separate conditions must be present—water,
bushes, trees, the tsetse-fly (*Glossina palpalis*),
and one infected person. Remove any one
of these and the curse is lifted. But let them
all be conjoined, and the sure destruction of
every human being in the district is only a
matter of time.

The Government of Uganda is now pursuing a policy based on the appreciation of
these facts. Wherever it is necessary to come
to the lake shores, as at Entebbe, Munyonyo,
Ripon Falls, Fajao, etc., the tsetse-fly is
banished or eliminated by cutting down the
trees, clearing away the bush, and planting in
its place the vigorous, rapid-growing *citronella*
grass, which, once firmly established, holds its
own against invading vegetation. Wherever
it is not possible to clear the shores of tsetse-
flies, they must be cleared of inhabitants.
And the extraordinary operation of moving
entire populations from their old homes to
new places—often against their will—has been
actually accomplished within the last year by
a combined dead-lift effort of these three
tremendous forces of Government which

regulate from such different points of view the
lives and liberties of the Baganda.

It does not follow that the lake shores will
have to be abandoned for ever. In a very
short time—some say two days, some eleven
hours—the infected tsetse is free from poison
and can no longer communicate it ; and once
the disease has been eradicated from the population, healthy people might return and be
bitten with impunity. Nor, on the other
hand, can we hope, unless some cure capable
of being applied on a large scale can be per-
fected, that the mortality in the immediate
future will sensibly diminish. For there are
many thousands of persons still affected,
and for these segregation, nursing, and compassion comprise the present resources of
civilization.

One thing is, however, above all things
important. There must be no losing heart.
At any moment the researches which are
being conducted in so many laboratories, and
in which Professor Koch has taken a leading
part, may produce an absolute therapeutic
remedy. By the administrative measures now
vigorously enforced it is believed that the
fatal contact between infected persons and

uninfected flies, between infected flies and uninfected persons, will have been effectively broken.   We cannot fail to learn more of the tsetse.   The humble black horse-fly, indistinguishable to the casual observer from harmless types, except that his wings are folded neatly like a pair of shut scissors, instead of splaying out on either side of his back, is now under a bright, searching, and pitiless eye.   Who are his enemies ?   What are his dangers ?   What conditions are essential to his existence ?   What conditions are fatal or inimical ?   International Commissions discuss him round green tables, grave men peer patiently at him through microscopes, active officers scour Central Africa to plot him out on charts.   A fine-spun net is being woven remorselessly around him.   And may not man find allies in this strange implacable warfare ? There are fishes which destroy mosquitoes, there are birds which prey upon flies, there are plants whose scent or presence is abhorrent or injurious to particular forms of insect life. In what places and for how long will the tsetse continue to fly, as he is wont, over the smooth, gleaming water, just above the reeds and bushes, just below the branches of the

THE GOVERNOR WITH BAGANDA GROUP.

overhanging trees ? *Glossina palpalis contra mundum !*

I have not sought to conceal the perils in describing the riches and the beauties of Uganda. The harsh contrasts of the land, its noble potentialities, its hideous diseases, its fecundity alike of life and death, are capable of being illustrated by many more facts and examples than I can here set down. But what an obligation, what a sacred duty is imposed upon Great Britain to enter the lists in person and to shield this trustful, docile, intelligent Baganda race from dangers which, whatever their cause, have synchronized with our arrival in their midst ! And, meanwhile, let us be sure that order and science will conquer, and that in the end John Bull will be really master in his curious garden of sunshine and deadly nightshade.

CHAPTER VI

KAMPALA

Two days after I had arrived at Entebbe the Governor took me over to Kampala. The distance between the ancient and the administrative capital is about twenty-four miles. The road, although unmetalled, runs over such firm, smooth sandstone, almost polished by the rains, that, except in a few places, it would carry a motor-car well, and a bicycle is 'an excellent means of progression. The Uganda Government motor-cars, which are now running well and regularly, had not then, however, arrived, and the usual method was to travel by rickshaw. Mounted in this light bicycle-wheeled carriage, drawn by one man between the shafts and pushed by three more from behind, we were able to make rather more than six miles an hour in very comfortable style.

The rickshaw-boys, who were neatly dressed

in white tunics and red caps, were relieved
every eight miles. They have their own way
of doing business. From the moment when
the travellers are seated in the rickshaw and
their labour begins, they embark upon an ever-
varying but absolutely interminable antiphony,
which, if it exhausts their breath, serves undoubtedly to keep their spirits up. " Burrulum," cry the pushers ; " Huma," says the
puller. " Burrulum," say the pushers again, and
so on over and over again for a very long time.
All these chaunts have their meanings, and if
the traveller is found to be heavy or known to
be ignorant of the language, he would not
always be complimented by a correct transla-
tion. The phrase I have quoted means " iron
upon wood "; and its signification is that the
iron of European strength and skill, however
superior, yet cannot get along without the
wood of native labour and endurance. With
such unexceptionable sentiments no one would
quarrel. Yet even these lose their flavour by
repetition, and after half an hour of " Burrulum " and " Huma " I was constrained to ask
the singers whether they could not possibly
manage to convey us in silence. They tried
their best, but I could see they were unhappy,

and after a while, out of compassion and to improve the pace, I withdrew the ban, and the chorus was joyfully resumed in a new and more elaborate form.

The manners of the Baganda are ceremonious to a degree. They well deserve Sir Harry Johnston's description of them as "the Japanese of Africa." If you say " Good morning " to a stranger on an English road, it is as like as not that his surprise will throw him into a posture of self-defence ; but when two Baganda meet they begin to salute each other as soon as they come within earshot. "How are you ? " cries the one. " Who am I that you should care to know ? " replies the other. " Humble though I be, yet I have dared," rejoins the first. " But say first how are *you*," continues the second. " The better for the honour you have done me," is the answer. By this they have already passed each other, and there is only time for the Parthian affability, "The honour is mine, and I shall treasure it," and a quavering of delicately-modulated, long-drawn " A—a—a's " of contentment and goodwill which gradually die away in the distance, leaving neither of them the worse circumstanced, nor the better

BAGANDA WARRIORS AT KAMPALA.

P. 106.

informed. I must add, for the reader's caution, that the aforesaid dialogue is not an invariable ritual. The phrases may be varied *ad infinitum* to suit the occasion ; but it will suffice as an illustration of these roadside courtesies.

If you wish to make a Baganda perfectly happy, all you need to do is to say, " Way wally," which means a sort of supremely earnest " Well done." The moment this talismanic expression has left your lips, the native to whom it is addressed will probably fall on his knees, and, clasping his two hands together, will sway them from side to side, as if he were playing a concertina, while all the time his face beams with a most benignant and compulsive smile, and he purrs, " A—o, a—o, a—o," as much as to say, " My cup of joy is overflowing." It is not in accordance with our ideas that man should kneel to man, and one feels uncomfortable to see it done. Yet it should not be thought that the action, as performed by the Baganda, involves or implies any servility. It is their good manners—and meant to be no more. Nor, once you are used to it, do they seem to lose at all in dignity. Only they win your heart.

The road from Entebbe to Kampala passes

through delicious country. Along its whole
length a double avenue of rubber trees has just
been planted, and behind these on each side
are broad strips of cotton plants, looking
beautiful with their yellow flowers or pinky-
white bolls. American upland cotton grown
in Uganda actually commands a higher price
in the Manchester market than when it is
grown in the United States. There appears
to be practically no natural difficulty in its
cultivation throughout the larger part of
Uganda. A great development is only a
question of organization and—money.

But I have forgotten that we have been
moving swiftly along the Kampala road, and
now we are almost in sight of the city.
Almost, but not quite; for, to tell the truth,
no one has ever seen Kampala. The traveller
sees the Government buildings and residences
neat and prim on one hill; he sees the King's
house and his Ministers' houses on another.
Upon a third, a fourth, or a fifth hill he may
discern successively the Protestant Cathedral,
the Catholic Mission, and the White Father's
Monastery. But Kampala, the home of sixty
thousand persons, is permanently invisible.
The whole town is buried under the leaves

KING DAUDI'S DRUMMERS AT KAMPALA.

P. 108.

WATCHING THE WAR-DANCE AT KAMPALA.
(Major Jenkins, Mr. Churchill, King Daudi, Sir H. Hesketh Bell.)

P. 104.

of innumerable banana plantations, which afford shade and food to its people, and amid which their huts are thickly scattered and absolutely concealed.

We were still three miles out of this "garden city" when the native reception began, and we travelled for a quarter of a mile between lines of white-robed Baganda, all mustered by their chiefs, and clapping their hands in sign of welcome. At last our procession of rickshaws reached a hillock by the roadside, at the top of which stood a pavilion, beautifully constructed of stout elephant grass like thin polished canes woven together with curious art. Down from this eminence, over a pathway strewn with rushes, came to meet us the King and his notables in a most imposing array. Daudi Chewa, the King or Kabaka of Uganda, is a graceful, distinguished-looking little boy, eleven years old. He was simply dressed in a flowing black robe edged with gold, and a little white gold-rimmed cap. Around him were the Council of Regency ; and at his right hand stood the Prime Minister, Sir Apolo Kagwar, a powerful, determined-looking man, wearing a crimson, gold-laced robe, on which shone many decorations, several British war medals, and the Order of St. Michael and St. George.

We all shook hands, and were then led up into the pavilion, where we took our seats on wicker chairs and ate sweet jellies while we conversed. The King, who is being most carefully educated by an English tutor, understands and speaks English quite well, but on this occasion he seemed too shy to say much more than " Yes " or " No," in a low, sweet drawl, and this formal interview soon came to an end.

The afternoon was consumed in ceremony; for the Commissioner of Uganda had to be sworn in the rank of Governor, to which he has been lately raised ; and there was a parade of troops, in which some five or six hundred very smart-looking soldiers took part, headed by the Kampala company of Sikhs. It was not until the shadows began to lengthen that we visited the Kabaka on the Royal Hill. He received us in his Parliament House. In this large and beautifully-constructed grass building about seventy chiefs and Baganda notables were assembled. The little Kabaka sat on his throne, and his subjects grouped themselves around and before him. We were

ON THE WAY TO KAMPALA.

ROAD BETWEEN JINJA AND LAKE CHIOGA.   P. 110.

given seats at his side, and the Prime Minister explained that the Baganda would show us the ceremony of swearing a chief. One of the most portly and dignified of the councillors thereupon advanced into the centre of the room, threw himself face downward on the ground, and poured out a torrent of asseverations of loyalty. After a few minutes he rose and began brandishing his spears, chaunting his oath all the while, until he had created an extraordinary appearance of passion. Finally he rushed from the building to go and slay the King's enemies outside. It was not until he returned a moment later, calm, sedate, and respectable, that I realized, from the merry smile on his face and from the mirth of the company, that he was "only pretending," and that the ceremony was merely a representation given to interest us.

The incident is remarkable because it illustrates the rapidity with which the Baganda people are leaving their past behind them. Already they laugh at their old selves. Ceremonies which twenty years ago had a solemn and awful significance, are to-day reproduced by this reflective people in much the same spirit as the citizens of Coventry revive the progress of Lady Godiva. The same thing happened at the war-dance the next day. Two or three thousand men, naked and painted for war, rushed frantically to and fro to the beating of drums and barbaric music, with every sign of earnestness and even frenzy. Yet a few minutes later they were laughing sheepishly at one another, and bowing to us like actors before the curtain, and the Prime Minister was making a speech to explain that this was meant to be a pageant of the bad old times reproduced for our benefit. Indeed, so unaccustomed to carry arms had the warriors become that not one in ten could find a spear to arm himself with, and they had to come with sticks and other stage-properties.

Even a comic element was provided in the shape of a warrior painted all over in a ridiculous manner, and held by two others with a rope tied round his middle. This, we were told, was "the bravest man in the army," who had to be restrained lest he should rush into battle too soon. It is not easy to convey the air of honest fun and good humour which pervaded these curious performances, or to measure the intellectual progress which the attitude of the Baganda towards them implied.

WAR DANCE AT KAMPALA.
"The bravest man in the army."

WAR DANCE AT KAMPALA. P. 112.

The Kabaka gave us tea in his house. It is a comfortable European building, quite small and modest, but nicely furnished, and adorned with familiar English prints and portraits of Queen Victoria and King Edward. Gradually he got the better of his shyness, and told me that he liked football more than anything else, and that his mathematical studies had advanced as far as " G.C.M.," initials which never fail to stir disagreeable school-day memories in my mind. He can write a very good letter in English, rides well on a nice pony, and will probably become a well-educated and accomplished man. Altogether it is a very pleasing spectacle to find in the heart of Africa, and amid so much barbarism, squalour, and violence, this island of gentle manners and peaceful civilization.

The next day was one unending pilgrimage. I have described how Kampala lies under the leaves of the plantain groves about the slopes of many hills. Each hill has its special occupants and purpose. Each of the different Christian missions has a hill to itself, and in the bad old days a Maxim gun was not thought at all an inappropriate aid to Christian endeavour. It would, however, be very

8

unfair to charge the missionaries with having created the feuds and struggles which convulsed Uganda twelve years ago. The accident that the line of cleavage between French and British influence was also the line of cleavage between Catholic and Protestant converts, imparted a religious complexion to what was in reality a fierce political dispute. These troubles are now definitely at an end. The arrival upon the scene of an English Catholic mission has prevented national rivalries and religious differences from mutually embittering one another. The erection of a stable Government and the removal of all doubts about the future of Uganda have led to an entire abatement of strife among devoted men engaged in a noble work. Not only is there peace among the different Christian missions themselves, but the Government of Uganda, so far from watching missionary enterprise with sour disfavour, is thoroughly alive to the inestimable services which have been and are daily being rendered by the missions to the native population, and excellent relations prevail.

In duty bound I climbed one hill after another and endeavoured to make myself

THE WHITE FATHERS' MISSION AT KAMPALA.

CHILDREN AT THE ENGLISH CATHOLIC MISSION, KAMPALA.

P. 114

acquainted with the details of mission work in Kampala. It comprises every form of moral and social activity. Apart from their spiritual work, which needs no advocacy here, the missionaries have undertaken and are now maintaining the whole educational system of the country. They have built many excellent schools, and thousands of young Baganda are being taught to read and write in their own language. The whole country is dotted with subsidiary mission stations, each one a centre of philanthropic and Christian effort. There are good hospitals, with skilful doctors and nurses or sisters of charity, in connection with all the missions. The largest of these, belonging to the Church Missionary Society, is a model of what a tropical hospital for natives ought to be. Technical education is now being added to these services, and in this, it is to be hoped, the Government will be able to cooperate. I do not know of any other part of the world where missionary influence and enterprise have been so beneficently exerted, or where more valuable results have been achieved.

On Namirembe Hill, where the Church Missionary Society have their head-quarters, a really fine cathedral, with three tall, quaint, thatched spires, has been built out of very primitive materials ; and this is almost the only building in Uganda which offers the slightest attempt at architectural display. Under the shadow of this I found myself on the afternoon of the 20th of November engaged in opening a high school for scholars who are more advanced than can be instructed in the existing establishments. A large and well-dressed audience, native and European, filled a good-sized room. The scholars crowded together in a solid mass of white-dressed youths upon the floor. The Kabaka and Sir Apolo Kagwar, who has himself five sons at the school, were upon the platform. The Governor presided. The Bishop made a speech. The schoolboys sang English songs and hymns in very good tune and rhythm. It was astonishing to look at the map of the British Empire hanging on the wall and to realize that all this was taking place near the north-western corner of the Victoria Nyanza.

It is eight miles from Kampala to Munyonyo, its present port on the lake, and this distance we covered in rickshaws over a shocking road. Munyonyo is itself little more than a jetty and

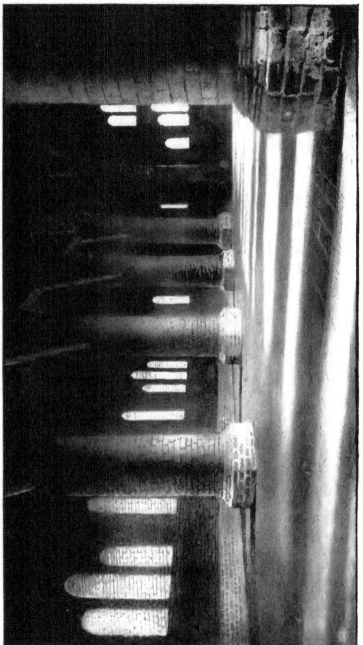

INTERIOR OF NAMIREMBE CATHEDRAL.

P. 116

a few sheds, but it affords a very good example of the salutary effects of cutting down the bush and forest. Mosquitoes and tsetses have been absolutely banished from the cleared area, and a place which a year ago was a death-trap is now perfectly safe and healthy. Plans are now on foot to make a new port a little farther along the coast at a point only five miles away from Kampala ; and when this has been connected with the capital, as it must be, by a line of mono-rail tramway, there is every reason to expect a substantial and growing trade.

The *Sir William Mackinnon*, a venerable vessel of the Uganda Marine, awaited our party, and we steamed off on the smooth waters of the lake, through an archipelago of beautiful islands—each one more inviting than the other—and all depopulated by sleeping sickness. All day long we voyaged in these sheltered waters, and in the evening the lights of Jinja guided us to our destination. One cannot help admiring the luck which led Speke to his thrilling discovery of the source of the Nile. There are five hundred gulfs and inlets on the northern shore of Lake Victoria, and nothing distinguishes this one from the

rest.   No current is perceptible to the ordinary
mariner until within a few miles of the rapids,
and although the presumption that so vast a
body of fresh water would have an overflow
somewhere had behind it a backing of strong
probability, the explorer might have searched
for a year without finding the spot.   Instead
of which he drifted and paddled gently along
until all of a sudden the murmur of a distant
cataract and the slight acceleration in the pace
of his canoe drew him to the long-sought birth-
place of the most wonderful river in the world.

It was dark when we landed at Jinja, and
I could not properly see the preparations made
for our reception by the local chiefs and the
Indian traders, of whom there was a considerable crowd.   The darkness, otherwise a cause
of disappointment, afforded the opportunity
for just the sort of brave act one so often finds
a British officer ready to do.   As the baggage
was being landed from the steamer on to the
jetty, a poor coolie slipped under his load, and
in an instant was engulfed in the deep black
waters below.   Whereupon, as a matter of
course, a young civilian in the Political Department jumped in after him in the darkness and
among the crocodiles, and fished him out safe

and sound, an act of admirable behaviour which
has since received the recognition of the Royal
Humane Society. I am not quite sure that
in all parts of Africa so high a standard of
honour and respect for the life of the humble
native would prevail.

Jinja is destined to become a very important
place in the future economy of Central Africa.
Situated at the point where the Nile flows out
of the Great Lake, it is at once on the easiest
line of water communication with Lake Albert
and the Soudan, and also where great water-
power is available. In years to come the
shores of this splendid bay may be crowned
with long rows of comfortable tropical villas
and imposing offices, and the gorge of the Nile
crowded with factories and warehouses. There
is power enough to gin all the cotton and saw
all the wood in Uganda, and it is here that
one of the principal emporia of tropical produce
will certainly be created. In these circumstances it is a pity to handicap the town with
an outlandish name. It would be much better
to call it Ripon Falls, after the beautiful
cascades which lie beneath it, and from
whose force its future prosperity will be
derived.

The Ripon Falls are, for their own sake, well worth a visit. The Nile springs out of the Victoria Nyanza, a vast body of water nearly as wide as the Thames at Westminster Bridge, and this imposing river rushes down a stairway of rock from fifteen to twenty feet deep, in smooth, swirling slopes of green water. It would be perfectly easy to harness the whole river and let the Nile begin its long and beneficent journey to the sea by leaping through a turbine. It is possible that nowhere else in the world could so enormous a mass of water be held up by so little masonry. Two or three short dams from island to island across the falls would enable, at an inconceivably small cost, the whole level of the Victoria Nyanza—over an expanse of a hundred and fifty thousand square miles—to be gradually raised six or seven feet ; would greatly increase the available water-power ; would deepen the water in Kavirondo Bay, so as to admit steamers of much larger draught ; and, finally, would enable the lake to be maintained at a uniform level, so that immense areas of swampy foreshore, now submerged, now again exposed, according to the rainfalls, would be converted either into clear water or dry land,

THE RIPON FALLS (Source of the Nile).

P. 120.

to the benefit of man and the incalculable destruction of mosquitoes.

As one watches the surging waters of the Ripon Falls and endeavours to compute the mighty energies now running to waste, but all within the reach of modern science, the problem of Uganda rises in a new form on the mind. All this water-power belongs to the State. Ought it ever to be surrendered to private persons? How long, on the other hand, is a Government, if not prepared to act itself, entitled to bar the way to others? This question is raised in a multitude of diverse forms in almost all the great dependencies of the Crown. But in Uganda the arguments for the State ownership and employment of the natural resources of the country seem to present themselves in their strongest and most formidable array. Uganda is a native State. It must not be compared with any of those colonies where there is a white population already established, nor again with those inhabited by tribes of nomadic barbarians. It finds its counterparts among the great native States of India, where Imperial authority is exercised in the name and often through the agency of a native prince and his own officers.

This combination of the external brain and
the native hand results in a form of government often highly acceptable to the general
body of the inhabitants, who are confronted
with no sudden or arbitrary changes in the
long-accustomed appearances of things. But
it involves all the administration of affairs in
a degree of complexity and delicacy which is
absent from simpler and cruder systems. In
such circumstances there cannot be much
opening for the push and drive of ordinary
commercial enterprise. The hustling business
man—admirably suited to the rough and
tumble of competitive production in Europe
or America—becomes an incongruous and
even a dangerous figure when introduced
into the smooth and leisurely development
of a native State. The Baganda will not be
benefited either morally or materially by contact with modern money-making or modern
money-makers. When a man is working only
for the profits of his company and is judged
by the financial results alone, he does not
often under the sun of Central Africa acquire
the best method of dealing with natives ; and
all sorts of difficulties and troubles will follow
any sudden incursion of business enterprise

into the forests and gardens of Uganda. And even if the country is more rapidly developed by these agencies, the profits will not go to the Government and people of Uganda, to be used in fostering new industries, but to divers persons across the sea, who have no concern, other than purely commercial, in its fortunes. This is not to advocate the arbitrary exclusion of private' capital and enterprise from Uganda. Carefully directed and narrowly controlled opportunities for their activities will no doubt occur. But the natural resources of the country should, as far as possible, be developed by the Government itself, even though that may involve the assumption of many new functions.

Indeed, it would be hard to find a country where the conditions were more favourable than in Uganda to a practical experiment in State Socialism. The land is rich; the people pacific and industrious. There are no great differences between class and class. One staple article of food meets the needs of the whole population, and produces itself almost without the aid of man. There are no European vested interests to block the way. Nowhere are the powers of the Government to regulate and direct the activities of the people more overwhelming or more comprehensive. The superiority of knowledge in the rulers is commanding. Their control upon the natives is exerted through almost every channel ; and besides the secular authorities —native and Imperial—there is the spiritual and educative influence of the missionaries to infuse human sympathy and moral earnestness into the regular machinery of State.

The first, and perhaps the greatest, difficulty which confronts the European Socialist is the choosing of Governors to whom the positively awful powers indispensable to a communistic society are to be entrusted. If a race of beings could be obtained when and as required from a neighbouring planet, whose practical superiority in virtue, science, wisdom, and strength was so manifest as to be universally acclaimed, this difficulty would disappear, and we might with composure await the decision of popular elections with all their defects and advantages. But in the absence of this dispensation the problem of how rulers are to be selected, and how, having been selected, they are to be controlled or changed, remains the first question of politics, even in days when the functions of government are, in general, restricted to the modest limits of *laissez-faire*.

In Uganda, however, this difficulty does not exist. A class of rulers is provided by an outside power as remote from and, in all that constitutes fitness to direct, as superior to the Baganda as Mr. Wells's Martians would have been to us. The British administration is in its *personnel* absolutely disinterested. The officials draw their salaries, and that is all. They have no end to serve, except the improvement of the country and the contentment of its people. By that test and that test alone are they judged. In no other way can they win approbation or fame. They are furthermore controlled in the exercise of their functions by a superior authority, specially instructed in this class of administration, and itself answerable to a Parliament elected on a democratic franchise. At no point in the whole chain of command is there any room for corruption, usurpation, or gross inefficiency.

It is clear that larger powers could be entrusted to the State in regard to the labour of its citizens than would ever be accorded to private employers. The subjects of every

European Power have accepted the obligation of military service to defend their respective countries from external attack. The Baganda, relieved from this harsh obsession, have no higher duty than to cultivate and develop the beautiful land they live in. And if it were desired to organize scientifically, upon a humane and honourable basis, the industry of an entire population, and to apply the whole fruits of their labour to their own enrichment and elevation, no better conditions are likely to be discovered than those which now exist in Uganda.

It might at any rate be worth while to make such an experiment, if only as a prelude to those more general applications of the principles of Socialism which are held in some quarters to be so necessary.

CHAPTER VII

'ON SAFARI'

Now the reader must really look at the map. To this point we have proceeded by train and steamer with all the power and swiftness of modern communication. If we have traversed wild and lonely lands, it has been in a railway carriage. We have disturbed the lion with the locomotive, and all our excursions have but led back to the iron road. But at Ripon Falls we are to let go our hold upon machinery. Steam and all it means is to be shut off. We are "to cut the painter," and, losing the impulsion of the great ship, are for a while to paddle about upon a vast expanse in a little cock-boat of our own. Back towards Mombasa, three days' journey will cover nine hundred miles. Forward, you will be lucky to make forty in the same time. Return at this moment is swift and easy. In a week it will be perhaps impossible. Going on means going through.

Everywhere great pathways are being cut into Africa. We have followed for nearly a thousand miles one leading from the East towards the centre. Far away from the North another line has been thrust forward by British efforts in peace and war. From Alexandria to Cairo, from Cairo to Wady Halfa, from Halfa to Berber, from Berber to Khartoum, from Khartoum to Fashoda, from Fashoda to Gondokoro, over a distance of nearly three thousand miles, stretches an uninterrupted service of trains and steamers. But between the landing-stage at Jinja and the landing-stage at Gondokoro there opens a wide gulf of yet unbridged, unconquered wilderness and jungle, across which and through which the traveller must crawl painfully and at a foot's pace, always amid difficulty and never wholly without danger. It is this gulf which we are now to traverse.

The distance from the Victoria to the Albert Nyanza is about two hundred miles in the direct line, and it is all downhill. The Great Lake is hoisted high above the highest hill-tops of England. From this vast elevated inland sea the descending Nile water flows through a channel of three thousand five

BETWEEN NIMULE AND GONDOKORO.

Capt. Read.   Mr. Marsh.   Dr. Goldie.   Mr. Ormsby.
Col. Wilson.   Mr. Churchill.   Capt Dickinson.   Lieut. Fishbourne, R.E.

P. 128.

hundred miles into the Mediterranean. The first and steepest stage of its journey is to the Albert Lake. This second body of water, which, except in comparison with the Victoria Nyanza, would be impressive—it is more than a hundred miles long—lies at an altitude of two thousand three hundred feet above the sea. So that in its first two hundred miles the Nile exhausts in the exuberant improvidence of youth about a third of the impulse which is to carry it through its venerable career. Yet this considerable descent of twelve hundred feet is itself accomplished in two short steps. There is one series of rapids, thirty miles long, below the Ripon Falls, and another of equal extent above the Murchison Falls. Between these two declivities long reaches of open river and the wide, level expanse of Lake Chioga afford a fine waterway.

Our journey from one great lake to the other divided itself therefore into three stages. Three marches through the forest to Kakindu, the first point where the Victoria Nile is navigable after the rapids; three days in canoes along the Nile and across Lake Chioga; and, lastly, five marches from the western end of Lake Chioga to the Albert Nyanza. Beyond

9

this, again, four days in canoes and steel sailing-boats, towed by a launch, would carry us to Nimule, where the rapids on the White Nile begin, and in seven or eight marches from there we should reach the Soudan steamers at Gondokoro. About five hundred miles would thus be covered in twenty days. It would take about the same time, if trains and steamers fitted exactly, to return by Mombasa and Suez to London.

Early in the morning of November 23rd our party set off upon this journey. Travelling by marches from camp to camp plays a regular part in the life of the average Central African officer. He goes " on Safari " as the Boer " on trek." It is a recognized state of being, which often lasts for weeks, and sometimes for months. He learns to think of ten days' " Safari " as we at home think of going to Scotland, and twenty days' " Safari " as if it were less than the journey to Paris. " Safari " is itself a Swahili word of Arabic origin, meaning an expedition and all that pertains to it. It comprises yourself and everybody and everything you take with you—food, tents, rifles, clothing, cooks, servants, escort, porters—but especially porters. Out of the range of steam

the porter is the primary factor. This ragged
figure, tottering along under his load, is the
unit of locomotion and the limit of possibility.
Without porters you cannot move. With
them you move ten or twelve miles a day, if
all is well. How much can he carry? How
far can he carry it? These are the questions
which govern alike your calculations and your
fate.

Every morning the porters are divided
into batches of about twenty, each under its
headman. The loads, which are supposed to
average about sixty-five pounds, are also
roughly parcelled out. As each batch starts
off, the next rushes up to the succeeding heap
of loads, and there is a quarter of an hour of
screaming and pushing—the strongest men
making a bee-line for the lightest-looking
loads, and being beaten off by the grim but
voluble headman, the weakest weeping feebly
beside a mountainous pile, till a distribution
has been achieved with rough justice, and the
troop in its turn marches off with indescribable
ululations testifying and ministering to the
spirit in which they mean to accomplish the
day's journey.

While these problems were being imperfectly

solved, I walked down with the Governor and one of the Engineer officers to the Ripon Falls, which are but half a mile from the Commissioner's house, and the sound of whose waters filled the air. Although the cataract is on a moderate scale, both in height and volume, its aspect—and still more its situation —is impressive. The exit or overflow of the Great Lake is closed by a natural rampart or ridge of black rock, broken or worn away in two main gaps to release the waters. Through these the Nile leaps at once into majestic being, and enters upon its course as a perfect river three hundred yards wide. Standing upon the reverse side of the wall of rock, one's eye may be almost on a plane with the shining levels of the Lake. At your very feet, literally a yard away, a vast green slope of water races downward. Below are foaming rapids, fringed by splendid trees, and pools from which great fish leap continually in the sunlight. We must have spent three hours watching the waters and revolving plans to harness and bridle them. So much power running to waste, such a coign of vantage unoccupied, such a lever to control the natural forces of Africa ungripped, cannot but vex and stimu-

FOREST SCENE NEAR RIPON FALLS.   P 133.

late imagination. And what fun to make the immemorial Nile begin its journey by diving through a turbine! But to our tale.

The porters had by now got far on their road, and we must pad after them through the full blaze of noon. The Governor of Uganda and his officers have to return to Entebbe by the steamer, so it is here I bid them good-bye and good luck, and with a final look at Ripon Falls, gleaming and resounding below, I climb the slopes of the river bank and walk off into the forest. The native path struck north-east from the Nile, and led into a hilly and densely wooded region. The elephant-grass on each side of the track rose fifteen feet high. In the valleys great trees grew and arched above our heads, laced and twined together with curtains of flowering creepers. Here and there a glade opened to the right or left, and patches of vivid sunlight splashed into the gloom. Around the crossings of little streams butterflies danced in brilliant ballets. Many kinds of birds flew about the trees. The jungle was haunted by game—utterly lost in its dense entanglements. And I think it a sensation all by itself to walk on your own feet, and staff in hand, along these mysterious paths, amid such beautiful, yet sinister, surroundings, and realize that one is really in the centre of Africa, and a long way from Piccadilly or Pall Mall.

Our first march was about fourteen miles, and as we had not started till the hot hours of the day were upon us, it was enough and to spare so far as I was concerned. Up-hill and down-hill wandered our path, now plunged in the twilight of a forest valley, now winding up the side of a scorched hill, and I had for some time been hoping to see the camp round every corner, when at last we reached it. It con- sisted of two rows of green tents and a large " banda," or rest-house, as big as a large barn in England, standing in a nice, trim clearing. These " bandas " are a great feature of African travel ; and the dutiful chief through whose territory we are passing had taken pains to make them on the most elaborate scale. He was not long in making his appearance with presents of various kinds. A lanky, black- faced sheep, with a fat tail as big as a pumpkin, was dragged forward, bleating, by two retainers. Others brought live hens and earthenware jars of milk and baskets of little round eggs. The chief was a tall, intelligent-looking man, with the winning

PALM TREE NEAR THE ASUA.

BANDA WITH ESCORT OF KING'S AFRICAN RIFLES.

P. 134.

smile and attractive manners characteristic of the country, and made his salutations with a fine air of dignity and friendship.

The house he had prepared for us was built of bamboo framework, supported upon a central row of Y-shaped tree-stems, with a high-pitched roof heavily thatched with elephant-grass, and walls of wattled reeds. The floors of African "bandas" when newly made are beautifully smooth and clean, and strewn with fresh green rushes; the interior is often cunningly divided into various apartments, and the main building is connected with kitchens and offices of the same unsubstantial texture by veranda-shaded passages. In fact, they prove a high degree of social knowledge and taste in the natives, who make them with almost incredible rapidity from the vegetation of the surrounding jungle; and the sensation of entering one of these lofty, dim, cool, and spacious interiors, and sinking into the soft rush-bed of the floor, with something to drink which is, at any rate, not tepid, well repays the glaring severities of a march under an Equatorial sun. The "banda," however, is a luxury of which the traveller should beware, for if it has stood for more than a week it becomes the home of innumerable insects, many of approved malevolence and venom, and spirillum fever is almost invariably caught from sleeping in old shelters or on disused camping-grounds.

Life " on Safari " is rewarded by a sense of completeness and self-satisfied detachment. You have got to " do " so many miles a day, and when you have " done " them your day's work is over. 'Tis a simple programme, which leaves nothing more to be demanded or desired. Very early in the morning, often an hour before daybreak, the bugles of the King's African Rifles sounded réveille. Every one dresses hurriedly by candle-light, eats a dim breakfast while dawn approaches ; tents collapse, and porters struggle off with their burdens. Then the march begins. The obvious thing is to walk. There is no surer way of keeping well in Uganda than to walk twelve or fourteen miles a day. But if the traveller will not make the effort, there are alternatives. There is the rickshaw, which was described in the last chapter—restful, but tedious ; and the litter, carried on the heads of six porters of different sizes, and shifted every now and then, with a disheartening jerk, to their shoulders and back

AN ENCAMPMENT.

P. 136.

again—this is quite as uncomfortable as it
sounds. Ponies cannot, or at least do not,
live in Uganda, though an experiment was
just about to be made with them by the Chief
of the Police, who is convinced that with
really careful stable management, undertaken
in detail by the owner himself, they could be
made to flourish. Mules have a better chance,
though still not a good one. We took one
with us on the last spell of " Safari " to Gondokoro, and were told it was sure to die ; but we
left it in apparently excellent condition and
spirits.

But the best of all methods of progression
in Central Africa—however astonishing it
may seem—is the bicycle. In the dry season
the paths through the bush, smoothed by the
feet of natives, afford an excellent surface.
Even when the track is only two feet wide,
and when the densest jungle rises on either
side and almost meets above the head, the
bicycle skims along, swishing through the
grass and brushing the encroaching bushes,
at a fine pace ; and although at every few
hundred yards sharp rocks, loose stones, a
water-course, or a steep hill compel dismount-
ing, a good seven miles an hour can usually

be maintained.   And think what this means.
From my own experience I should suppose
that with a bicycle twenty-five to thirty miles
a day could regularly be covered in Uganda,
and, if only the porters could keep up, all
journeys could be nearly trebled, and every
white officer's radius of action proportionately
increased.

Nearly all the British officers I met already
possessed and used bicycles, and even the
native chiefs are beginning to acquire them.
But what is needed to make the plan effective
is a good system of stone, fumigated, insect-
proof rest-houses at stages of thirty miles
on all the main lines of communication.
Such a development would mean an enormous
saving in the health of white officials and a
valuable accession to their power.   Had I
known myself before coming to Uganda the
advantages which this method presents, I
should have been able to travel far more
widely through the country by the simple ex-
pedient of trebling the stages of my journeys,
and sending porters on a week in advance to
pitch camps and deposit food at wide intervals.
And then, instead of merely journeying from
one Great Lake to the other, I could, *within*

the same limits of time, have explored the fertile and populous plateau of Toro, descended the beautiful valley of the Semliki, and traversed the Albert Lake from end to end, and skirted the slopes of Ruenzori. " If youth but knew . . . ! "

But the march, however performed, has its termination; and if, as is recommended, you stop to breakfast and rest upon the way, the new camp will be almost ready upon arrival. During the heat of the day every one retires to his tent or to the more effective shelter of the " banda," to read and sleep till the evening. Then as the sun gets low we emerge to smoke and talk, and there is, perhaps, just time for the energetic to pursue an antelope, or shoot a few guinea-fowl or pigeons.

With the approach of twilight comes the mosquito, strident-voiced and fever-bearing; and the most thorough precautions have to be taken against him and other insect dangers. We dine in a large mosquito-house made entirely of fine gauze, and about twelve feet cubically. The bedding, which should if possible be packed in tin boxes, is unrolled during the day, and carefully protected by mosquito-nets well tucked in, against all forms of vermin.   Every one puts on mosquito-boots—long, soft, leather leggings, reaching to the hips.   You are recommended not to sit on cane-bottomed chairs without putting a newspaper or a cushion on them, to wear a cap, a scarf, and possibly gloves, and to carry a swishing mosquito-trap.   Thus one moves, comparatively secure, amid a chorus of ferocious buzzings.

To these precautions are added others. You must never walk barefoot on the floor, no matter how clean it is, or an odious worm, called a " jigger," will enter your foot to raise a numerous family and a painful swelling. On the other hand, be sure when you put on boots or shoes that, however hurried, you turn them upside down and look inside, lest a scorpion, a small snake, or a perfectly frightful kind of centipede may be lying in ambush. Never throw your clothes carelessly upon the ground, but put them away at once in a tin box, and shut it tight, or a perfect colony of fierce-biting creatures will beset them.   And, above all, quinine ! To the permanent resident in these strange countries no drug can be of much avail; for either its protection is diminished with habit, or the doses have to be increased to impossible limits. But the traveller, who is passing through on a journey of only a few months, may recur with safety and with high advantage to that admirable prophylactic. Opinions differ as to how it should be taken. The Germans, with their love of exactness even in regard to the most uncertain things, prescribe thirty grains on each seventh day and eighth day alternately. We followed a simpler plan of taking a regular ten grains every day, from the moment we left Port Said till we arrived at Khartoum. No one in my party suffered from fever even for a day during the whole journey.

Our second day's march was about the same in length and character, except that we were nearer the river, and as the path led through the twilight of the forest we saw every now and then a gleam of broad waters on our left. At frequent intervals—five or six times during the day—long caravans of native porters were met carrying the produce of the fertile districts between Lake Chioga and Mount Elgon into Jinja. Nothing could better show the need of improved communications than this incipient and potential trade—ready to begin and thrusting forward along bush-paths on the heads of tottering men. For the rest, the country near the river seemed the densest and most impenetrable jungle, hiding in its recesses alike its inhabitants and its game.

The third morning, however, brought us among "shambas," as the patches of native cultivation are called; and the road was among plantations of bananas, millet, cotton, castor-oil, and chilies. Here in Usoga, as throughout Uganda, the one staple crop is the banana; and as this fruit, when once planted, grows and propagates of its own accord, requiring no thought or exertion, it finds special favour with the improvident natives, and sustains them year after year in leisured abundance, till a sudden failure and a fearful famine restore the harsh balances of the world.

After a tramp of twelve miles, and while it was still comparatively early—for we had started before dawn—we reached Kakindu. The track led out of the forest of banana-groves downwards into more open spaces and blazing sunlight, and there before us was the Nile. Already—forty miles from its source, near four thousand from its mouth—it was a noble river: nearly a third of a mile in breadth of clear, deep water rolling forward majestically between banks of foliage and verdure. The " Chioga flotilla," consisting of the small steam launch, *Victoria*, a steel boat, and two or three dug-out canoes, scooped out of tree-trunks, awaited us ; and after the long, hot business of embarking the baggage and crowding the native servants in among it, was completed, we parted from our first relay of escorts and porters, and drifted out on the flood.

The next three days of our life were spent on the water—first cruising down the Victoria Nile till it flows into Chioga, and then traversing the smooth, limpid expanses of that lake. Every evening we landed at camps prepared by the·Busoga chiefs, pitched our tents, lighted our fires, and erected our mosquito-houses, while dusk drew on, and thunderstorms— frequent at this season of the year—wheeled in vivid splendour about the dark horizon. All through the hot hours of the day one lay at the bottom of massive canoes, sheltered from the sun by an improvised roof of rushes and wet grass. From time to time a strange bird, or, better still, the rumour of a hippo— nose just peeping above the water—enlivened the slow and sultry passage of the hours; and one great rock, crowded with enormous crocodiles, all of whom—a score at least—leaped together into the water at the first shot, afforded at least one really striking spectacle.

As the Victoria Nile approaches Lake Chioga, it broadens out into wide lagoons, and the sloping banks of forest and jungle give place to unbroken walls of papyrus-reeds, behind which the flat, surrounding country is invisible, and above which only an isolated triangular hill may here and there be descried, purple in the distance.   The lake itself is about fifty miles long from east to west, and eleven broad, but its area and perimeter are greatly extended by a series of long arms, or rather fingers, stretching out in every direction, but especially to the north, and affording access by water to very wide and various districts.   All these arms, and even a great part of the centre of the lake, are filled with reeds, grass, and water-lilies, for Chioga is the first of the great sponges upon which the Nile lavishes its waters.   Although a depth of about twelve feet can usually be counted on, navigation is impeded by floating weeds and water-plants; and when the storms have swept the northern shore, numerous papyrus-tangled islands, complete with their populations of birds and animals, are detached, and swim erratically about the lake to block accustomed channels and puzzle the pilot.

For one long day our little palpitating launch, towing its flotilla of canoes, plashed through this curious region, at times winding through a glade in the papyrus forest scarcely a dozen yards across, then presently emerging into wide flood, stopping often to clear our propeller from tangles of accumulating greenery. The middle of the lake unrolls large expanses of placid water. The banks and reeds recede into the distance, and the whole universe becomes a vast encircling blue globe of sky and water, rimmed round its middle by a thin band of vivid green. Time vanishes, and nothing is left but space and sunlight.

All this while we must carefully avoid the northern, and particularly the north-western shore, for the natives are altogether unadministered, and nearly all the tribes are hostile. To pursue the elephants which, of course (so they say), abound in these forbidden precincts is impossible; to land for food or fuel would be dangerous, and even to approach might

10

draw a splutter of musketry or a shower of
spears from His Majesty's yet unpersuaded
subjects.

The Nile leaves the north-west corner of the
lake at Namasali and flows along a broad
channel above a mile in width, still enclosed
by solid papyrus walls and dotted with floating
islands. Another forty miles of steaming and
we reach Mruli. Mruli is a representative
African village. Its importance is more
marked upon the maps than on the ground.
An imposing name in large black letters calls
up the idea of a populous and considerable
township. All that meets the eye, however,
are a score of funnel-shaped grass huts, surrounded by dismal swamps and labyrinths of
reeds, over which clouds of mosquitoes danced
feverishly. A long wattled pier had been built
from terra firma to navigable water, but the
channel by which it could be approached had
been wholly blocked by a floating island, and
this had to be towed painfully out of the way
before we could land. Here we were met by
a fresh escort of King's African Rifles, as spick
and span in uniform, as precise in their military
bearing, as if they were at Aldershot ; by a mob
of fresh porters, and, lastly, by the only friendly

LANDING AT MRULI.

P. 146.

tribe from the northern bank of the river : and while tents were pitched, baggage landed, and cooking-fires began to glow, these four hundred wild spearmen, casting aside their leopard skins, danced naked in the dusk.

CHAPTER VIII

Murchison Falls

WE had intended, on leaving the Nile where it turns northward at Mruli, to march directly across to Hoima, on the Albert Lake; and this journey, by way of Masindi, would have required four marches. But tales of the beauty and wonder of the Murchison Falls had captivated my mind, and before embarking at Kakindu a new plan had been resolved. Runners were sent back to the telegraph wire at Jinja, and thence a message was flashed by Kampala to Hoima, directing the flotilla which awaited us there, to steam to the north end of the Albert and meet us by the foot of the Murchison Falls at Fajao. Thither we were now to proceed by five marches—two to Masindi and three more turning northward to the Nile.

The road from Mruli consists of a sort of embanked track through low-lying and desolate scrub and jungle. The heavy black cotton soil, cracked and granulated by the heat, offered at this time a hardened if uneven surface to the bicycle; but in the rains such paths must become utterly impassable. As one advances westward the country improves rapidly in aspect. The dismal flats of the South Chioga shore are left behind, and the traveller discovers more characteristic Uganda scenery in a region of small hills and great trees. Before Masindi is reached we are again in a rich and beautiful land. Pools of shining water, set in verdant green, flash back the sunbeams. Bold bluffs and ridges rise on all sides from amid the unceasing undulations of the ground. Streams plash merrily downwards through rocky channels. The yellow grass roofs of frequent villages peep from underneath their groves of bananas among broad streaks of cultivated ground, and chiefs and headmen salute the stranger with grave yet curious politeness as the long "safari" winds beneath the trees.

The heat grows as the altitude dwindles, and even in the early morning the sun sits hard and heavy on the shoulders. At ten o'clock its power is tremendous. So long as the roadway consisted of nobbly lumps of black cotton soil bicycling, though possible in places, was scarcely pleasant. But the change in the landscape arises from the change in the soil. The fields are now of bright red earth, the paths of red sandstone washed in places almost as smooth and as firm as asphalt by the rains and sparkling with crystalline dust ; and when the ridges which form the watershed between Lake Chioga and Lake Albert had been topped, my bicycle glided almost without impulsion down four miles of gradual descent into Masindi. This station—which is the residence of a collector—lies embosomed in a wide bay of gently-sloping hills clothed with noble trees. It is indeed a pleasant' spot. There are real houses, standing on high stone platforms, with deep verandas and wire gauze windows. The roads are laid out in bold geometry of broad red lines. There are avenues of planted trees, delicious banks of flowers, a prepared breakfast, *cold*, not cool, drinks, a telegraph office, and a file of the *Times*. What more could an explorer desire or the Fates accord ?

We were now to strike northwards to the Nile at Fajao in three long marches (for the

porters) of about sixteen miles each. Upon
the Hoima road some preparations had been
made to make the journey easier by clearing
the encroaching jungle from the track and
constructing rest-houses. But my change of
plan had disconcerted these arrangements, and
on the new route we had to clear our own
paths from the overgrowth by which even in
a season, if unused, they are choked, and to
trust to tents and improvised shelters. Progress was therefore slow and camps unpretentious. But all was redeemed by the wonders
of the scene.

For a whole day we crept through the
skirts of the Hoima forest, amid an exuber-
ance of vegetation which is scarcely describ-
able. I had travelled through tropical forests
in Cuba and India, and had often before
admired their enchanting, yet sinister, luxuriance. But the forests of Uganda, for mag-
nificence, for variety of form and colour,
for profusion of brilliant life—plant, bird,
insect, reptile, beast—for the vast scale and
awful fecundity of the natural processes that
are beheld at work, eclipsed, and indeed
effaced, all previous impressions. One becomes,
not without a secret sense of aversion, the

spectator of an intense convulsion of life and death. Reproduction and decay are locked struggling in infinite embraces. In this glittering Equatorial slum huge trees jostle one another for room to live ; slender growths stretch upwards—as it seems in agony— towards sunlight and life. The soil bursts with irrepressible vegetations. Every victor, trampling on the rotting mould of exterminated antagonists, soars aloft only to encounter another host of aerial rivals, to be burdened with masses of parasitic foliage, smothered in the glorious blossoms of creepers, laced and bound and interwoven with interminable tangles of vines and trailers. Birds are as bright as butterflies ; butterflies are as big as birds. The air hums with flying creatures ; the earth crawls beneath your foot. The telegraph-wire runs northward to Gondokoro through this vegetable labyrinth. Even its poles had broken into bud !

As we advanced, continually rising or falling with the waves of the land, and moving in rapid alternations from a blazing patch of sunshine into a cloistered dimness, every now and then the path became smooth, broad, and of firm sandstone. And here one could watch the columns of marching soldier-ants. Perhaps in a hundred yards the road would be crossed four times by these fierce armies. They move in regular array, and upon purposes at once inscrutable and unswerving. A brown band, perhaps two inches broad and an inch and a half *deep*, is drawn across your track. Its ends are lost in the recesses of the jungle. It moves unceasingly and with a multiplied rapidity; for each ant runs swiftly forward, whether upon the ground or upon the backs of his already moving comrades. About a yard away, on each side of the main column, are the screening lines of the flank-guards, and for five yards beyond this every inch is searched, every object is examined by tireless and fearless reconnoitring patrols. Woe to the enemy who is overtaken by these hordes. No matter what his size or nature, he is attacked at once by an ever-increasing number of assailants, each one of whom, upon remorseless instinct, plunges his strong mandibles in the flesh, and will have his head pulled off his shoulders rather than let go.

These ant armies fascinated me. I could not resist interfering with them. With my walking-stick I gently broke the column and pushed the swarming rope off its line of march. Their surprise, their confusion, their indignation were extreme. But not for an instant did they pause. In a second the scouts were running all over my boots eagerly seeking an entry, and when I looked back from this to the walking-stick I held it was already alive. With a gesture so nimble that it might have been misunderstood, I cast it from me and jumped back out of the danger circle until I found refuge on a large rock at a respectful distance. The Soudanese sergeant-major of the escort, a splendid negro, drilled as smart as a Grenadier Guardsman and with a good long row of medal ribbons on his khaki tunic, so far forgot himself as to grin from ear to ear. But his gravity was fully restored when I invited him to rescue my walking-stick, which lay abandoned on the field in the mandibles of the victorious enemy. The devoted man was, however, equal to the crisis.

I have a sad tale also to tell of the perversity of butterflies. Never were seen such flying fairies. They flaunted their splendid liveries in inconceivable varieties of colour and pattern in our faces at every step. Swallow-tails, fritillaries, admirals, tortoise-shells, peacocks, orange-tips—all executed in at least a dozen novel and contrasted styles, with many even more beautiful, but bearing no resemblance to our British species—flitted in sunshine from flower to flower, glinted in the shadow of great trees, or clustered on the path to suck the moisture from any swampy patch. The butter-fly is a dirty feeder, and if ever some piece of putrescent filth lay odorous on the ground, be sure it would be covered with a cloud of these greedy insects, come in such gay attire to eat such sorry meat. I found them sometimes so intoxicated with feasting that I could pick them up quite gently in my fingers without the need of any net at all.

To any one who has ever tried to collect the modest and now all too rare and scattered butterflies of Britain, these sights could not but be a hard temptation. For a week I had resisted it, not because it was not easy enough to make a net, but because of the difficulty of setting and preserving the prizes ; and it was not until the end of our first day's march out from Masindi that I was told that much the best way of sending butterflies home from Africa was to enclose them in neatly-folded triangles of paper and leave them to be set in London. Forthwith, out of telegraph-wire and mosquito-curtain, a net was made, and before another dawn I was fully equipped. It is almost incredible to state that from that very moment, except near the Murchison Falls, I scarcely ever saw a really fine butterfly again all the way to Gondokoro. Whether this was due to the intelligent perversity of these insects, or to the fact that we had left the deeper recesses of 'the forest region, I do not inquire; but the fact remains, and I carry away from the butterflies of Uganda only the haunting memories of unrealized opportunity.

This first day's march from Masindi was a long one, and our porters panted and toiled under their loads through the heat of the day. It was not till the afternoon that the main body came into camp, and stragglers trickled through into the dusk. Meanwhile the local natives built under our eyes, with extraordinary speed and cleverness, a spacious dining-hall and two or three quite excellent bedrooms from the surrounding elephant-grass and bamboo groves; and we fared as comfortably in these two humble dwellings as if we dwelt in kings' palaces. The forest was a little thinner on the second day, although the jungle was of the same dense and tangled fertility. We started an hour before sunrise, and by eight o'clock had climbed to the saddle of the high rocky wall which contains the valley of the Victoria Nile. From this elevation of, perhaps, six hundred feet above the general level of the plain a comprehensive view of the landscape was for the first time possible. In every direction spread a wide sea of foliage, thinning here into bush, darkening there into forest, rising and falling with the waves of the land, and broken only by occasional peaks of rock. Far away to the north-west a long silver gleam, just discernible through the haze of the horizon, revealed to our eyes the distant prospect of the Albert Nyanza. The camera cannot do justice to such a panorama. In photographs these vast expanses look like mere scrubby commons, inhospitable and monotonous to the eye, melancholy to the soul. One has to remember that here are Kew Gardens and the Zoo combined on an unlimited scale; that Nature's central productive laboratory is here working night and day at full blast; and that the scrubby common of the picture is really a fairyland of glades and vistas, through which an army of a hundred thousand men might march without the glint of a bayonet, or even the dust of an artillery column, betraying their presence to the watcher on the crag.

Our camp this night lay in a tiny patch cleared in the heart of this wild world.   The cluster of tents under a canopy of palms, illumined by the watch-fires, bright with lanterns, and busy with the moving figures of men and the hum of human activity, seemed at a hundred yards' distance an island of society amid an ocean of Nature.   To what strange perils—apart altogether from the certainty of losing your way—would a walk of a quarter of a mile in any direction expose the wanderer ? To withdraw from the firelight was to be engulfed in the savage conditions of prehistoric time.   Advance, and the telegraph-wire would tell you the latest quotations of the London markets, the figures of the newest by-election. An odd sensation !

We had scarce proceeded for an hour on our third march, when just as it grew daylight a low vibrant murmur began to be perceptible in the air.   Now it was lost as we descended

MURCHISON FALLS.

into some moist valley, now it broke even more strongly on the ear as we reached the summit of some ascent—the sound of the Nile plunging down the Murchison Falls. And by nine o'clock, when we were still about ten miles off, a loud, insistent, and unceasing hum had developed. These Falls are certainly the most remarkable in the whole course of the Nile. At Foweira the navigable reaches stretching from Lake Chioga are interrupted by cataracts, and the river hurries along in foam and rapid down a gradual but continuous stairway, enclosed by rocky walls, but still a broad flood. Two miles above Fajao these walls contract suddenly till they are *not six yards apart*, and through this strangling portal, as from the nozzle of a hose, the whole tremendous river is shot in one single jet down an abyss of a hundred and sixty feet.

The escarpment over which the Nile falls curves away in a vast bay of precipitous, or almost precipitous, cliffs, broken here and there by more gradual rifts, and forms the eastern wall of the Albert Lake, from whose waters it rises abruptly in many places to a height of six or seven hundred feet. Arrived at the verge of this descent, the lower reaches of the

Victoria Nile could be discerned, stretching away mile after mile in a broad, gleaming ribbon almost to its mouth on the lake. The Falls themselves were, indeed, invisible, concealed behind a forested bluff, but their roaring left no doubt of their presence. Below me a zigzag path led down by long descents to the water's edge, and on an open meadow a row of tents and grass houses had already been set up.

Fajao as a native town was no more. At hardly any point in Uganda has the sleeping sickness made such frightful ravages. At least six thousand persons had ˏperished in the last two years. Almost the whole population had been swept away. Scarcely enough remained to form the deputation, who, in their white robes, could be distinguished at the entrance to the cleared area of the camping-ground. And this cleared area was itself of the utmost importance; for all around it the powers of evil were strong. The groves which fringed and overhung the river swarmed with tsetse flies of newly-replenished venom and approved malignity, and no man could enter them except at a risk. After pausing for a few minutes to watch a troop of baboons who

FAJAO, WITH NATIVES ASSEMBLED TO WELCOME US.

P. 160.

were leaping about from tree to tree on the
opposite hill, and who seemed as big as men,
I climbed down the zigzag, photographed the
deputation, and shook hands with the chief.
He was a very civilized chief—by name James
Kago—who wore riding-breeches and leather
gaiters, and who spoke a few unexpected
sentences of excellent English. He seemed in
the best of spirits, and so did the remnant of
the population who gathered behind him,
though whether this was due to stoical philo-
sophy or good manners, I could not tell. All
was smiles and bows and gurglings of guttural
gratification. The district officer who had
travelled with me explained that the chief
had had the path up to the top of the Falls
improved, and that he proposed, after we had
lunched and rested, to guide us along it to
the very edge of the abyss, but that the forest
along the river-bank was so dangerous because
of the tsetses that we should in prudence wear
veils and gloves before entering it. With all
of this I made no quarrel.

In a little rocky inlet forming a small
natural harbour we found the Albert flotilla
already arrived. It consisted of the *Kenia*,
a steam-launch about forty feet long, decked,

11

and with a cabin, and drawing four feet of water, and three steel sailing-boats of different sizes—to wit, the *James Martin*, the *Good Intent*, and the *Kisingiri*. These small vessels were to carry us down the Victoria Nile into the Albert Nyanza, across the top end of this lake, and then down the hundred and seventy miles' reach of the White Nile till navigation is barred at Nimule by more cataracts. They were manned by a crew of jolly Swahili tars smartly dressed in white breeches and blue jerseys, on whose breasts the words "Uganda Marine" were worked in yellow worsted. The engineer of the steam-launch commanded the whole with plenary powers of discipline and diplomacy; and it was by means of this little group of cock-boats that trade and communications with the Nile province and around the whole of Lake Albert were alone maintained. The flotilla, nestling together in its harbour and sheltered by a rocky break-water from the swift current, made a pretty picture; and behind it the Nile, streaked and often covered with the creamy foam of the Falls, swept along in majestic flood six hundred yards from brim to brim.

We began our climb to the summit of the

FLOTILLA AT FAIAO

P. 162.

Falls in the blazing heat of the day, and for
the first time I was forced to confess the
Central African sun as formidable as that
which beats on the plains of India. Yet even
at the worst moments it is more endurable,
for the breeze does not stifle you with the
breath of a furnace. First the path led through
the deadly groves; and here, of course, the
most beautiful butterflies—some five inches
across the wings—floated tantalizingly. Sometimes we descended to where the river lapped
along the rocks and curled in eddies under
floating islands of froth. Precautions were
required against diverse dangers. The Nile
below the Murchison Falls swarms with crocodiles, some of an enormous size, and herds of
hippopotamus are found every half mile or
so; so that, what with the rifles which it was
necessary to take for great beasts, and the
gloves and veils which were our protection
against even more villainous small ones, we
were painfully encumbered. Indeed, the veils
were such a nuisance and the heat was so
great that I resolved to hazard the tsetse and
took mine off. But after half an hour of
menacing buzzings, and after a fly—presumably
of the worst character—had actually settled

on my shoulder, brushed off by the promptness of my companion, I changed my mind again.

As we were thus scrambling along the brink of the river a crocodile was discovered basking in the sunshine on a large rock in mid-stream, about a hundred and fifty yards from the shore. I avow, with what regrets may be necessary, an active hatred of these brutes and a desire to kill them. It was a tempting shot, for the ruffian lay sleeping in the sun-blaze, his mouth wide open and his fat and scaly flanks exposed. Two or three attendant white birds hopped about him, looking for offal, which I have been assured (and does not Herodotus vouch for it ?) they sometimes pick from his very teeth. I fired. What the result of the shot may have been I do not know, for the crocodile gave one leap of mortal agony or surprise and disappeared in the waters. But then it was my turn to be astonished. The river at this distance from the Falls was not broader than three hundred yards, and we could see the whole shore of the opposite bank quite plainly. It had hitherto appeared to be a long brown line of mud, on which the sun shone dully. At the sound of the

The Top of the Murchison Falls.

Uganda Scenery.   P. 164.

shot the whole of this bank of the river, over
the extent of at least a quarter of a mile,
sprang into hideous life, and my companions
and I saw hundreds and hundreds of crocodiles, of all sorts and sizes, rushing madly into
the Nile, whose waters along the line of the
shore were lashed into white foam, exactly as
if a heavy wave had broken. It could be
no exaggeration to say that at least a thousand
of these saurians had been disturbed at a
single shot. Our British friends explained
that Fajao was the favourite haunt of
the crocodiles, who lay in the water below
the Falls waiting for dead fish and animals
carried over by the river. Very often, they
told us, hippos from the upper river and from
Lake Chioga were caught and swept downwards, the force of the water " breaking every
bone in their body. " Indeed," added the
officer, somewhat obscurely, " they are *very
lucky* if they are not smashed into pulp."

At length we turned a corner and came
face to face with the Falls. They are wonderful to behold, not so much because of their
height — though that is impressive — but
because of the immense volume of water
which is precipitated through such a narrow

outlet.   Indeed, seeing the great size of the
river below the Falls, it seemed impossible to
believe that it was wholly supplied from this
single spout.   In clouds of rainbow spray and
amid thunderous concussions of sound we
set to work to climb the southern side of the
rock wall, and after an hour achieved the
summit.   It was possible to walk to within an
inch of the edge and, lying on one's face
with a cautious head craned over, to look
actually down upon the foaming hell beneath.
The narrowness of the gorge at the top had
not been overstated.   I doubt whether it is
fifteen feet across from sheer rock to sheer
rock.   Ten pounds, in fact, would throw an
iron bridge across the Nile at this point. ' But
it is evident that the falling waters must have
arched and caved away the rock below their
surface in an extraordinary degree, for otherwise there could not possibly be room for the
whole river to descend.

We waited long at this strange place, watching the terrible waters, admiring their magnificent fury, trying to compute their force.
Who can doubt that the bridle is preparing
which shall hold and direct their strength,
or that the day will come when forlorn

Fajao—now depopulated and almost dere-lict—will throb with the machinery of manu-facture and electric production ? I cannot believe that modern science will be content to leave these mighty forces untamed, unused, or that regions of inexhaustible and un-equalled fertility, capable of supplying all sorts of things that civilized industry needs in greater quantity every year, will not be brought—in spite of their insects and their climate—into cultivated subjection. Certain it is that the economy of the world remains hopelessly incomplete while these neglects prevail, and, while it would be wasteful and foolish to hustle, it would be more wasteful and more foolish to abate the steady progress of development.

From these reflections I was roused abruptly by the Nile, a wave of whose tur-bulent waters—cast up by some unusual commotion as they approached the verge—boiled suddenly over a ledge of rock hitherto high and dry, carrying an ugly and perhaps indignant swish of water to my very feet.

CHAPTER IX

HIPPO CAMP

IT took no little time to stow all our baggage, food and tents upon the launch and its steel boats, and though our camp was astir at half-past three, the dawn was just breaking when we were able to embark. And then the *James Martin* wedged herself upon a rock a few yards from the shore of the sheltering inlet, and seemed to have got herself hard and fast; for pull as we might with all the force of the launch at full steam, and the added weight of the current to help us, not an inch would she budge. Everything had, therefore, to be unloaded again from the straggler, and when she had thus been lightened and her freight transferred to the attendant canoes, James Kago ordered his tribesmen to leap into the water, which was not more than five feet deep, and push and lift the little vessel whilst the steamer tugged. But this task the natives

THE LANDING-PLACE AT FAIAO.

P. 160.

were most reluctant to perform out of fear of the crocodiles, who might at any moment make a pounce, notwithstanding all the noise and clatter. Thereupon the energetic chief seized hold of them one after another round the waist, and threw them full-splash into the stream, till at least twenty were accumulated round the boat, and then, what with their impatience to finish their uncomfortable job and our straining tow rope, the *James Martin* floated free, was reloaded, and we were off.

As we drifted out into mid-stream the most beautiful view of the falls broke upon us. It was already almost daylight, but the sun had not yet actually topped the great escarpment over which the Nile descends. The banks on both sides of the river, clad with dense and lofty forest and rising about twice as high as Cliveden Woods from the water's edge, were dark in shadow. The river was a broad sheet of steel grey veined with paler streaks of foam. The rock portals of the falls were jetty black, and between them, illumined by a single shaft of sunlight, gleamed the tremendous cataract— a thing of wonder and glory, well worth travelling all the way to see.

We were soon among the hippopotami.

Every two or three hundred yards, and at every bend of the river, we came upon a herd of from five to twenty.   To us in a steam launch they threatened no resistance or danger.   But their inveterate hostility to canoes leads to repeated loss of life among the native fishermen, whose frail craft are crumpled like eggshells in the snap of enormous jaws.   Indeed, all the way from here to Nimule they are declared to be the scourge and terror of the Nile.   Fancy mistaking a hippopotamus—almost the largest surviving mammal in the world—for a water lily.   Yet nothing is more easy.   The whole river is dotted with floating lilies detached from any root and drifting along contentedly with the current.   It is the habit of the hippo to loll in the water showing only his eyes and the tips of his ears, and perhaps now and again a glimpse of his nose, and thus concealed his silhouette is, at three hundred yards, almost indistinguishable from the floating vegetation. I thought they also looked like giant cats peeping.   So soon, however, as they saw us coming round a corner and heard the throbbing of the propeller, they would raise their whole heads out of the water to have a look, and then immediately dive to the bottom in disgust.

EARLY MORNING ON THE NILE AT FAJAO.

FAJAO. P. 170.

Our practice was then to shut off steam and drift silently down upon them. In this way one arrives in the middle of the herd, and when curiosity or want of air compels them to come up again there is a chance of a shot. One great fellow came up to breathe within five yards of the boat, and the look of astonishment, of alarm, of indignation, in his large, expressive eyes—as with one vast snort he plunged below —was comical to see. These creatures are not easy to kill. They bob up in the most unexpected quarters, and are down again in a second. One does not like to run the risk of merely wounding them, and the target presented is small and vanishing. I shot one who sunk with a harsh sort of scream and thud of striking bullet. We waited about a long time for him to float up to the surface, but in vain, for he must have been carried into or under a bed of reeds and could not be retrieved.

The Murchison, or Karuma, Falls, as the natives call them, are about thirty miles distance from the Albert Lake, and as with the current we made six or seven miles an hour, this part of our journey was short. Here the Nile offers a splendid waterway. The main channel is at least ten feet deep, and navigation, in spite of shifting sandbanks, islands, and entanglements of reeds and other vegetation, is not difficult. The river itself is of delicious, sweet water, and flows along in many places half-a-mile broad. Its banks for the first twenty miles were shaded by beautiful trees, and here and there contained by bold headlands, deeply scarped by the current. The serrated outline of the high mountains on the far side of the Albert Nyanza could soon be seen painted in shadow on the western sky. As the lake is approached the riparian scenery degenerates; the sandbanks became more intricate; the banks are low and flat, and huge marshes encroach upon the river on either hand. Yet even here the traveller moves through an imposing world.

At length, after five or six hours' steaming, we cleared the mouth of the Victoria Nile and swam out on to the broad expanses of the lake. Happily on this occasion it was quite calm. How I wished then that I had not allowed myself to be deterred by time and croakers from a longer voyage, and that we could have turned to the south and, circumnavigating the Albert, ascended the Semliki river with all its mysterious attractions, have visited the forests on the south-western shores, and caught, perhaps, a gleam of the snows of Ruenzori! But we were in the fell grip of carefully-considered arrangements, and, like children in a Christmas toy shop always looking back, were always hurried on.

Yet progress offered its prizes as well as delay. Some of my party had won the confidence of the engineer of the launch, who had revealed to them a valuable secret. It appeared that "somewhere between Lake Albert and Nimule "—not to be too precise— there was a place known only to the elect, and not to more than one or two of them, where elephants abounded and rhinoceros swarmed. And these rhinoceros, be it observed, were none of your common black variety with two stumpy horns almost equal in size, and a prehensile tip to their noses. Not at all; they were what are called " white " rhino—Burchell's white rhinoceros,[1] that is their full style—with one long, thin, enormous horn, perhaps a yard

---

[1] "I am informed by the courtesy of Mr. Lydekker of the British Natural History Museum, that the true name of the white rhinoceros found in Uganda is *Rhinoceros Simus Cottoni.* 'Burchell's white rhinoceros' is the designation of the southern race; but I have preserved in the text the name commonly used in Uganda."

long—on their noses, and with broad, square upper lips.   Naturally we were all very much excited, and in order to gain a day on our itinerary to study these very rare and remarkable animals more closely, we decided not to land and pitch a camp, but to steam on all through the night.   Meanwhile our friend the engineer undertook to accomplish the difficult feat of finding the channel, with all its windings, in the dark.

The scene as we left the Albert Lake and entered the White Nile was of surpassing beauty.   The sun was just setting behind the high, jagged peaks of the Congo Mountains to the westward.   One after another, and range behind range, these magnificent heights—rising perhaps to eight or nine thousand feet—unfolded themselves in waves of dark plum-coloured rock, crested with golden fire.   The lake stretched away apparently without limit like the sea, towards the southward in an ever-broadening swell of waters—flushed outside the shadow of the mountains into a delicious pink.   Across its surface our tiny flotilla—four on a string—paddled its way towards the narrowing northern shores and the channel of the Nile.

APPROACH TO LAKE ALBERT, WITH THE CONGO HILLS IN
THE DISTANCE.

WADELAI.   P. 174.

The White Nile leaves the Albert Lake in
majesty. All the way to Nimule it is often
more like a lake than a river. For the first
twenty miles of its course it seemed to me to
be at least two miles across. The current is
gentle, and sometimes in the broad lagoons
and bays into which the placid waters spread
themselves it is scarcely perceptible. I slept
under an awning in the *Kisingiri*, the last and
smallest boat of the string, and, except for the
native steersman and piles of baggage, had it
all to myself. It was, indeed, delightful to lie
fanned by cool breezes and lulled by the sooth-
ing lappings of the ripples, and to watch, as it
were, from dreamland the dark outlines of the
banks gliding swiftly past and the long moonlit
levels of the water.

At daybreak we were at Wadelai. In
twenty-four hours from leaving Fajao we had
made nearly a hundred miles of our voyage.
Without the sigh of a single porter these small
boats and launch had transported the whole of
our " safari " over a distance which would on
land have required the labours and sufferings
of three hundred men during at least a week
of unbroken effort. Such are the contrasts
which impress upon one the importance of

utilising the water-ways of Central Africa, of establishing a complete circulation along them, and of using railways in the first instance merely to link them together.

Wadelai was deserted. Upon a high bank of the river stood a long row of tall, peaked, thatched houses, the walls of a fort, and buildings of European construction. All was newly abandoned to ruin. The Belgians are evacuating all their posts in the Lado enclave except Lado itself, and these stations, so laboriously constructed, so long maintained, will soon be swallowed by the jungle. The Uganda Government also is reducing its garrisons and administration in the Nile province, and the traveller sees, not without melancholy, the spectacle of civilization definitely in retreat . after more than half a century of effort and experiment.

We disembarked and climbed the slopes through high rank grass and scattered boulders till we stood amidst the rotting bungalows and shanties of what had been a bold bid for the existence of a town. Wadelai had been occupied by white men perhaps for fifty years. For half a century that feeble rush-light of modernity, of cigarettes, of newspapers, of whisky and pickles, had burned on the lonely banks of the White Nile to encourage and beckon the pioneer and settler. None had followed. Now it was extinguished; and yet when I surveyed the spacious landscape with its green expanses, its lofty peaks, its trees, its verdure, rising from the brink of the mighty and majestic river, I could not bring myself for a moment to believe that civilization has done with the Nile Province or the Lado Enclave, or that there is no future for regions which promise so much.

All through the day we paddled prosperously with the stream. At times the Nile lost itself in labyrinths of papyrus, which reproduced the approaches to Lake Chioga, and through which we threaded a tortuous course, with many bumps and brushings at the bends. But more often the banks were good, firm earth, with here and there beautiful cliffs of red sandstone, hollowed by the water, and rising abruptly from its brim, crowned with luxuriant foliage. In places these cliffs were pierced by narrow roadways, almost tunnels, winding up to the high ground, and perfectly smooth and regular in their construction. They looked as if they

12

were made on purpose to give access to and
from the river; and so they had been—by the
elephants. Legions of water-fowl inhabited
the reeds, and troops of cranes rose at the
approach of the flotilla. Sometimes we saw
great, big pelican kind of birds, almost as big
as a man, standing contemplative on a single
leg, and often on the tree-tops a fish-eagle,
glorious in bronze and cream, sat sunning
himself and watching for a prey.

I stopped once in the hope of catching
butterflies, but found none of distinction—only
a profuse variety of common types, a high
level of mediocrity without beauties or commanders, and swarms of ferocious mosquitoes
prepared to dispute the ground against all
comers; and it was nearly four in the afternoon
when the launch suddenly jinked to the left
out of the main stream into a small semi-
circular bay, five hundred yards across, and
we came to land at " Hippo Camp."

We thought it was much too late to attempt
any serious shooting that day. There were
scarcely three and a half hours of daylight.
But after thirty-six hours cramped on these
little boats a walk through jungle was very
attractive; and, accordingly, dividing our-

THE "KENIA," "JAMES MARTIN," AND "GOOD HOPE"
NEARING NIMULE.

HIPPO CAMP. P. 178.

selves into three parties, we started in three
different directions—like the spokes of a wheel.
Captain Dickinson, who commanded the
escort, went to the right with the doctor;
Colonel Wilson and another officer set out
at right angles to the river bank; and I went
to the left under the guidance of our friend
the engineer. I shall relate very briefly what
happened to each of us. The right-hand party
got, after an hour's walking, into a great herd
of elephants, which they numbered at over
sixty. They saw no very fine bulls; they
found themselves surrounded on every side
by these formidable animals; and, the wind
being shifty, the hour late, and the morrow free,
they judged it wise to return to camp without
shooting. The centre party, consisting of
Colonel Wilson and his companion, came
suddenly, after about a mile and a half's
walk, upon a fine solitary bull elephant.
They stalked him for some time, but he
moved off, and, on perceiving himself followed,
suddenly, without the slightest warning on his
part and no great provocation on theirs, he
threw up his trunk, trumpeted, and charged
furiously down upon them; whereupon they
just had time to fire their rifles in his face

and spring out of his path. This elephant was followed for some miles, but it was not for three months afterwards that we learned that he had died of his wounds and that the natives had recovered his tusks.

So much for my friends. Our third left party prowled off, slanting gradually away inland from the river's bank. It was a regular wild scrub country, with high grass and boulders and many moderate-sized trees and bushes, interspersed every hundred yards or so by much bigger ones. Near the Nile extensive swamps, with reeds fifteen feet high, ran inland in long bays and fingers, and these, we were told, were the haunts of white rhino. We must have walked along warily and laboriously for nearly three-quarters of an hour, when I saw through a glade at about two hundred yards distance a great dark animal. Judging from what I had seen in East Africa, I was quite sure it was a rhinoceros. We paused, and were examining it carefully with our glasses, when all of a sudden it seemed to treble in size, and the spreading of two gigantic ears—as big, they seemed, as the flaps of French windows—proclaimed the presence of the African elephant. The next

moment another and another and another
came into view, swinging leisurely along
straight towards us—and the wind was almost
dead wrong.

We changed our position by a flank march
of admirable celerity, and from the top of a
neighbouring ant-bear hill watched, at the
distance of about one hundred and fifty yards,
the stately and awe-inspiring procession of
eleven elephants. On they came, loafing
along from foot to foot—two or three tuskers
of no great merit, several large tuskless
females, and two or three calves. On the
back of every elephant sat at least one beautiful white egret, and sometimes three or four,
about two feet high, who pecked at the tough
hide—I presume for very small game—or surveyed the scene with the consciousness of
pomp. These sights are not unusual to the
African hunter. Those who dwell in the
wilderness are the heirs of its wonders. But
to me I confess it seemed a truly marvellous
and thrilling experience to wander through
a forest peopled by these noble Titans, to
watch their mysterious, almost ghostly, march,
to see around on every side, in large trees
snapped off a few feet from the ground, in

enormous branches torn down for sport, the
evidences of their giant strength.   And then,
while we watched them roam down towards
the water, I heard a soft swishing sound
immediately behind us, and turning saw, not
forty yards away, a splendid full-grown rhinoceros, with the long, thin horn of his rare
tribe upon him—the famous white rhinoceros
—Burchell himself—strolling placidly home
after his evening drink and utterly unconscious
of the presence of stranger or foe !

We had very carefully judged our wind in
relation to the elephants.   It was in consequence absolutely wrong in relation to the
rhinoceros.   I saw that in another fifty yards
he would walk right across it.   For my own
part, perched upon the apex of a ten-foot ant-
bear cone, I need have no misgivings.   I was
perfectly safe.   But my companions, and the
native orderlies and sailors who were with us,
enjoyed no such security.   The consequences
of not killing the brute at that range and with
that wind would have been a mad charge
directly through our party.   A sense of responsibility no doubt restrained me ; but I
must also confess to the most complete astonishment at the unexpected apparition.   While

MR. CHURCHILL ON THE OBSERVATION LADDER AT HIPPO CAMP.

BANK OF THE VICTORIA NILE. P. 182.

I was trying to hustle the others by signals and whispers into safer places ; the rhino moved steadily, crossed the line of wind, stopped behind a little bush for a moment, and then, warned of his danger, rushed off into the deepest recesses of the jungle. I had thrown away the easiest shot I ever had in Africa. Meanwhile the elephants had disappeared.

We returned with empty hands and beating hearts to camp, not without chagrin at the opportunity which had vanished, but with the keenest appetite and the highest hopes for the morrow. Thus in three hours and within four miles of our landing-place our three separate parties had seen as many of the greatest wild animals as would reward the whole exertion of an ordinary big-game hunt. As I dropped off to sleep that night in the little *Kisingiri*, moored in the bay, and heard the grunting barks of the hippo floating and playing all around, mingling with the cries of the birds and the soft sounds of wind and water, the African forest for the first time made an appeal to my heart, enthralling, irresistible, never to be forgotten.

At the earliest break of day we all started in the same order, and with the sternest resolves.

During the night the sailors had constructed out of long bamboo poles a sort of light tripod, which, serving as a tower of observation, enabled us to see over the top of the high grass and reeds, and this proved of the greatest convenience and advantage, troublesome though it was to drag along. We spent the whole morning prowling about, but the jungle, which twelve hours before had seemed so crowded with game of all kinds, seemed now utterly denuded. At last, through a telescope from a tree-top, we saw, or thought we saw, four or five elephants, or big animals of some kind, grazing about two miles away. They were the other side of an enormous swamp, and to approach them required not only traversing this, but circling through it for the sake of the wind.

We plunged accordingly into this vast maze of reeds, following the twisting paths made through them by the game, and not knowing what we might come upon at every step. The ground under foot was quite firm between the channels and pools of mud and water. The air was stifling. The tall reeds and grasses seemed to smother one; and above, through their interlacement, shone the full blaze of the noonday sun. To wade and waddle through such country carrying a double-barrelled ·450 rifle, not on your shoulder, but in your hands for instant service, peering round every corner, suspecting every thorn-bush, for at least two hours, is not so pleasant as it sounds. We emerged at last on the farther side under a glorious tree, whose height had made it our beacon in the depths of the swamp, and whose far-spreading branches offered a delicious shade.

It was three o'clock. We had been toiling for nine hours and had seen nothing—literally nothing. But from this moment our luck was brilliant. First we watched two wild boars playing at fighting in a little glade—a most delightful spectacle, which I enjoyed for two or three minutes before they discovered us and fled. Next a dozen splendid water-buck were seen browsing on the crest of a little ridge within easy shot, and would have formed the quarry of any day but this; but our ambition soared above them, and we would not risk disturbing the jungle for all their beautiful horns. Then, thirdly, we came slap up against the rhinoceros. How many I am not certain—four, at least. We had actually walked past them as they stood sheltering under the trees. Now, here they were, sixty yards away to the left rear—dark, dim, sinister bodies, just visible through the waving grass.

When you fire a heavy rifle in cold blood it makes your teeth clatter and your head ache. At such a moment as this one is almost unconscious alike of report and recoil. It might be a shot-gun. The nearest rhino was broadside on.   I hit him hard with both barrels, and down he went, to rise again in hideous struggles—head, ears, horn flourished agonizingly above the grass, as if he strove to advance, while I loaded and fired twice more. That was all I saw myself. Two other rhinos escaped over the hill, and a fourth, running the other way, charged the native sailors carrying our observation tower, who were very glad to drop it and scatter in all directions.

To shoot a good specimen of the white rhinoceros is an event sufficiently important in the life of a sportsman to make the day on which it happens bright and memorable in his calendar. But more excitement was in store for us before the night. About a mile from the spot where our victim lay we stopped to rest and rejoice, and, not least, refresh. The

MR. CHURCHILL AND BURCHELL'S WHITE RHINOCEROS.

P. 186.

COLONEL WILSON'S ELEPHANT.

THE "KENIA," "JAMES MARTIN," AND "GOOD HOPE"
ON THE WHITE NILE.

P. 187.

tower of observation—which had been dragged so painfully along all day—was set up, and, climbing it, I saw at once on the edge of the swamp no fewer than four more full-grown rhinoceros, scarcely four hundred yards away. A tall ant-hill, within easy range, gave us cover to stalk them, and the wind was exactly right. But the reader has dallied long enough in this hunter's paradise. It is enough to say that we killed two more of these monsters, while one escaped into the swamp, and the fourth charged wildly down upon us and galloped through our party without apparently being touched himself or injuring any one. Then, marking the places where the carcasses lay, we returned homeward through the swamp, too triumphant and too tired to worry about the enraged fugitives who lurked in its recesses. It was very late when we reached home, and our friends had already hewn the tusks out of a good elephant which Colonel Wilson had shot, and were roasting a buck which had conveniently replenished our larder.

Such was our day at Hippo Camp, to which the ardent sportsman is recommended to repair, when he can get some one to show him the way.

CHAPTER X

DOWN THE WHITE NILE

WE lingered lovingly around Hippo camp
for two more days, moving to other lagoons
and overflows of the river with the launch,
and striking out inland in search of the great
herd of elephants. But although their recent
presence was on all sides proclaimed by
snapped-off trees and trampled ground, and
broad lanes cut through the grass, we saw
none of them; and a tribe of natives who
helped to carry home a variety of buck one
afternoon,. informed us upon expert authority
that the whole herd-had been alarmed by the
arrival of strangers and the sound of firing,
and had retired three days' journey from the
river's bank. These natives — of the Lado
Enclave — were gentleman-like folk, and I
parleyed long with them upon their affairs.
They were stark naked and very dignified,
with graceful athletic bodies, long tapering

188

well-bred hands, and bright keen eyes. The local chief exhibited all these characteristics in a superior degree, and his natural pre-eminence was recognized with instantaneous obedience by his followers. We loaded them with gifts. First, quantities of meat and hides; then chocolate all round — they love sweet things—three pieces of sugar for each, at least one empty bottle per man, and tin pots and card-board boxes almost without limit. The chief showed a fine taste in all these things, and annexed at once in the Imperial style whatever took his fancy, to whomsoever it belonged. I cast about for some means of doing him especial honour, and luckily remembered that I had bought a Japanese *kimono* for a dressing-gown in passing through Port Said on the journey out. With this he was forthwith enrobed, and I must say he assumed the flowing garment with that easy grace and natural self-possession which are the gifts of a wilderness life. Thus the fabrics of Cathay were by the enterprise of Europe introduced into the heart of Africa.

When, finally, with much reluctance we left this attractive place and pushed off determinedly into the stream, we lost no time in

making Nimule. Steaming throughout the
night and all next day along a broad flood
contained by high and healthy slopes—now
clothed with forest, now with waving grass—
we approached, at about four in the afternoon,
the mountains beneath which is the administrative station of Nimule. Hitherto the course
of the Nile since it left the Albert Lake had
been smooth and open—a broad, steady-flow-
ing river everywhere navigable to vessels of not
more than four feet draught. But at Nimule,
after a reach of more than a hundred and
seventy miles of unobstructed waterway, the
river turns a sharp right angle and enters a
long succession of granite gorges, through
which it plunges in ceaseless cataract for a
hundred and twenty miles. It is here at the
head of these rapids that one of the great
reservoirs of the Upper Nile must some day
be constructed. " I spent hours," said Sir
William Willcocks, the " practical mystic "
of hydraulic engineering, " looking at the site,
and seeing in a vision a great regulating work
of the future." And indeed the exact scientific
control of the whole vast system of Central
African waters, of the levels of every lake, of
the flow of every channel, from month to

month and from day to day throughout the
year, is a need so obvious and undisputed
as to leave argument unemployed.

The change in the character of the river
separated us finally from our flotilla. From
Nimule to Gondokoro we must again proceed
by land, and the swift and easy progress of the
last few days must be exchanged for the steady
grind of marches. It was this stage which had
always been painted to me as the most dangerous and unhealthy in our whole journey,
and I had pictured to myself eight days of toil
through swamp and forest amid miasma and
mosquitoes. These anticipations were not sus-
tained. Of the disadvantages of the track
along the river bank I cannot speak ; but the
upper road over the hills is certainly excellent
and healthy, and runs throughout over firm
dry undulations of a bright, breezy, scrub-
covered country.

At Nimule we touched the telegraph wire
again, and from the Reuter's accumulations
which I studied, I learned that Parliament
would not meet till the 19th of January. This
gave another ten days' more rope, and I began
to realize how much the spirit of these wonderful lands had taken possession of me, for it

was only with the greatest reluctance and
difficulty, that I forced myself to continue my
homeward journey without first turning back
with the launch and circumnavigating Lake
Albert.   No exertion or inconvenience seemed
too great to win a few more glimpses of these
enchanted seas and gardens, on which I may
perhaps not look again, but from whose spell I
can never be free.   Porters to be fed from day
to day, the Sirdar's steamer waiting at the
Soudan frontier, public meetings looming
heavily in the far-off distance, drove me
onward ; and with feelings of keen and genuine
regret we addressed ourselves to the march
to Gondokoro.

This was accomplished uneventfully in six
stages, three of which were double marches.
The country was pleasant and healthy, the
scenery imposing, and, under a fierce sun, the
air was cool.   Each morning we started before
dawn, and by noon had camped by the side of
one of the tributary rivers or streams which
flow into the Nile.   Of these the Asua was
the most important, and the picture of the
long *safari* fording it and coming into camp
among the palm-trees of the southern bank is
one which lingers pleasantly in my memory.

P. 192.

FORDING THE ASUA.

But this I must say—somehow after Nimule the charm was broken, and none of the regions through which the traveller passes in the long-drawn descent of the Nile revive in any degree those delicious sensations of wonder and novelty which are associated with the great lakes and the kingdoms of Uganda, Usoga, and Unyoro, to say nothing of what I have not been fortunate enough to see — Toro, Ankole, the Semliki, and the Mountains of the Moon.

At the end of the sixth day we arrived at Gondokoro. The last march had been long and scorching. The moisture seemed to have gone from the air, and the vegetation, abundant though it was, seemed parched and stunted. The approaches to Gondokoro are beset by a herd of three hundred elephants of peculiar ill-fame. Nearly all the eligible tuskers have been killed. The females and young bulls are fierce and wary, and, taught by frequent contact with the white man, and protected by the sacred game laws, exercise a lawless and tyrannical power over the whole region. On every side their depredations are to be seen. Great trees pushed over in careless sport, native plantations trampled into

13

ruin, the roads rendered precarious for the traveller, the mails often interrupted for days at a time, and occasional loss of life, are the features of this domination.   And it seems likely to last a long time, for I was informed that the young bulls would not be sufficiently grown for about forty years, and even then, as the two white officers in the station are not allowed to shoot more than one elephant a-piece each year, the nuisance will only gradually be abated.

Rogue elephants are of course fair game at any time, and the day before we arrived at Gondokoro, the young civil officer of the station had encountered one in a manner which he was scarcely likely to forget. For, having pursued this evil-doer for some time, he at last got into an excellent position, and was about to fire at a distance of thirty yards when suddenly the elephant, without even trumpeting rushed furiously upon him, and, paying no attention to the two heavy bullets which struck him in the head, chased the officer twice round an uncommonly small bush; and then, distracted by the spectacle of the native gun-bearer in flight, turned off after this new prey, and, overtaking the poor wretch, smashed him to pieces with one blow of his terrible trunk. " Cet animal est très méchant ; quand on l'attaque, il se défend." We reached the bungalow, which serves as the seat of government, in time to see the tusks of this man-slayer, who had died of his wounds, brought in by the tribe whose plantations he had so often ravaged.

Gondokoro, like most of the names which figure so imposingly upon the African map, is not a numerously populated town. There are about six houses and a number of native huts. There is, however, a telegraph station, a prison, a court-house, and the lines of a company of native police and King's African Rifles. Here the Nile again becomes navigable, and offers an unbroken waterway open to large vessels until the Shabluka cataract is reached, a hundred miles below Khartoum and fifteen hundred miles from Gondokoro. And here at the river's bank, seen through a tracery of palms, were the white funnel and superstructure of the Sirdar's steamer with all the letters and newspapers ; and which, instead of pursuing us across Uganda, had " come through the other way."

" Had come through the other way "—it is

an easy phrase to write : but how much it signifies in the modern history of Africa ! Ten or eleven years ago this journey which I was now able to make so easily, so prosperously, so comfortably, would have been utterly impossible. The Dervish empire, stretching from Wady Halfa or Abu Hamed to Wadelai, interposed a harsh barrier which nothing but a stricken field could sweep away ; and these long reaches of the Nile which now bore a fleet of fifty steamers were silent in the embrace of a devastating barbarism. A grim slaughter which had strewn the sands of Kerreri, twelve hundred miles to the North, with *jibba*-clad corpses " like snow-drifts " had blasted a passage, and the Nile was free.

Embarked at Gondokoro we passed out of the sphere of the Colonial Office into the domain of that undefined joint authority which regulates the Soudan, which flies two flags side by side on every public building, and which you can only correspond with through the British Foreign Office.

Henceforward our journey was comfortable, and regular. Yet though I had no official work to do and was merely coming home the shortest way, I could not traverse the Soudan

THE BELGIAN OFFICIALS AT LADO.

GONDOKORO. P. 196.

without the keenest interest. When one has started from Cairo and padded up the Nile to Wady Halfa, crossed the desert railway to the Atbara, marched thence two hundred miles to the battle of Omdurman, one feels one has seen something of the Nile. Yet now we had followed it the other way from its source for nearly five hundred miles, and yet twelve hundred more intervened before even Omdurman was reached ; and as the mighty and peerless river unrolled its length and immemorial history, the feelings of reverence, without which no traveller can drink its sweet waters, grew in intensity.

I yield to no one in recognition of the constructive and reconstructive work which Sir Reginald Wingate and his able officers have, with scanty means and in spite of grave military dangers, wrought in the Soudan. Yet it is not possible to descend the Nile continuously from its source at Ripon Falls without realizing that the best lies behind one. Uganda is the pearl. The Nile province and the Lado Enclave present splendid and alluring panoramas. Even the march from Nimule to Gondokoro is through a fertile and inspiring region. But thereafter the beauty dies out of the landscape and the richness from the land.   We leave the regions of abundant rainfall, of Equatorial luxuriance, of docile peoples, of gorgeous birds and butter-flies and flowers.   We enter stern realms of sinister and forbidding aspect, where nature is cruel and sterile, where man is fanatical and often rifle-armed.   Cultivation—nay, vegeta-tion, is but a strip along the river bank : and even there thorn-bushes and prickly aloes are its chief constituents.   We enter two successive deserts as contrasted in their character, as redoubtable in their inhospitality, as Dante's Circles of the Inferno: the Desert of Sudd and the Desert of Sand.

About a hundred miles from Gondokoro the White Nile enters and spills itself in a vast and appalling swamp.   Of the action of this tremendous sponge, whether beneficial in regulating the flow, or harmful in wasting the water through evaporation, nothing need here be said.   But its aspect is at once so dismal and so terrifying that to travel through it is a weird experience.   Our steamer, with the favouring current, made at least seven miles an hour, and, as the moon was full, we travelled night and day.   For

REVIEW AT KHARTOUM.

SOUDAN GOVERNMENT STEAMER " DAL."

P. 198.

three days and three nights we were continuously in this horrible swamp into which the
whole of the United Kingdom could be easily
packed. By day from the roof of the high
pilot-house a commanding view revealed hour
after hour, in every direction, one uninterrupted ocean of floating vegetation spreading
to far horizons. The papyrus-plant is in itself
a beautiful, graceful, and venerable thing.
To travel through the *sudd*, is to hate it for
evermore. Rising fifteen feet above the level
of the water, stretching its roots twenty or
even thirty feet below, and so matted and
tangled together that elephants can walk safely
upon its springy surface, papyrus is the beginning and end of this melancholy world. For
hundreds of miles nothing else is to be
perceived—not a mountain-ridge blue on the
horizon, scarcely a tree, no habitation of man,
no sign of beast. The silence is broken only
by the croaking of innumerable frog armies,
and the cry of dreary birds.

The vigorous operations of the *sudd*-cutters
have opened, and the constant traffic of steamers
has preserved and improved, a channel about a
hundred yards wide, winding by loops and
corkscrews through the swamp. The river

presents a depth of thirty feet along this course, and greater vessels could thread its length for nearly a thousand miles. The navigation is intricate and peculiar. Indeed, it would seem to be an art by itself. No effort is made by the Arab pilots, who alone are employed, to avoid collisions with the banks. On the contrary, they rely upon them as an essential feature of their management of the steamer. The vessel bumps regularly at almost every corner from one cushion of *sudd* to the other, or plunges its nose into the reeds and waits for the currents to carry its stern round, bumps again and recovers its direction. Sometimes where the twists were very sharp we would turn completely round, not once but two or three times, and our movements round an S-curve were even more complicated. The bumps occasionally swept us out of our chairs and sent us sprawling on the deck. In this strange fashion we waltzed along at full speed for about seventy or eighty hours.

Meanwhile the Nile was accomplishing its destiny. Its vast tributary rivers, the Sobat and the Bahr-el-Ghazal, came to reinforce its flow. The miles spread out behind us in a long succession of hundreds. At length the *sudd* expanses begin to contract. Distant mountains rise against the steel-blue sky in serrated silhouette, and gradually draw in upon the river. Islands of earth and trees, peaks of sharp rock break here and there the awful monotony of waving reeds. At last the banks become firm and clear-cut walls of yellow sand, fringed in places with palms and shady trees, and everywhere bristling with undergrowth of thorns. We leave the wilderness of moisture, we approach the wilderness of drought. But first, in a middle region, vast areas of dusty scrub-covered plains, not wholly incapable of cultivation in the rainy season, supporting always flocks and herds, now flank both sides of the river. The camel caravans pad slowly across them under the blaze and glitter of the heat. The mirage begins to twist and blur the landscape with deceptive waters. At intervals of forty or fifty miles are the stations of the Soudan Government, each trim and regular with its public buildings, its storehouses, the lines of beehive huts of its garrison, a tangle of native sailing-craft, and always, or nearly always, one or two white gunboats of war-time days now turned policemen of the river.

Thus we reach in time Fashoda—now called Kodok for old sake's sake ; and here are clusters of Shillooks who (by request) stand pensively on one leg in their natural attitude, and smart companies of Soudanese troops and British officers, civil and military—the whole clear-cut under sun-blaze dry light, veiled only in dancing dust-devils piteously whipped by strong hot winds. All this was like a piece of the Omdurman campaign to me—the old familiar Soudan, so often made known to British minds by pen, pencil, and photograph during nearly twenty years of war, unfolded itself feature by feature. Yet we were still five hundred miles south of Khartoum!

At Meshra-er-Zeraf we stopped for two days to shoot, by the Sirdar's invitation, in the extensive game reserve, and were fortunate in securing a buffalo and various antelope. We wandered through a harsh country, of white sand and tussocks of coarse grass, more grey than green, with leafless black thorn-trees densely tangled ; yet it seemed full of game. In three hours' walk on the second morning I shot a fine waterbuck, two reed-bucks, and two of a beautiful herd of roan antelope, who walked slowly down to water past our ambus-

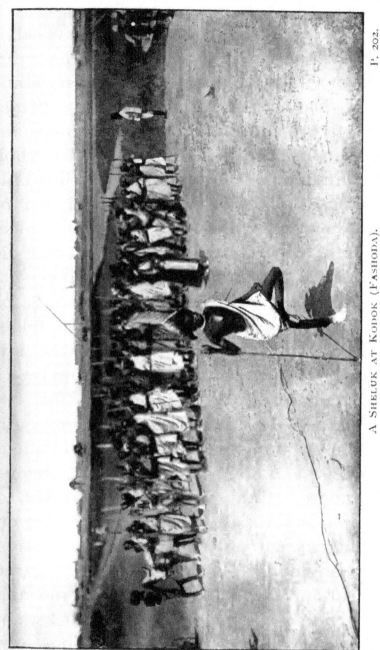

A Sheluk at Kodok (Fashoda).

P. 202.

cade. And, be it remembered, that the pleasure and excitement of such sport are in these
lands always heightened by the possibility that
at any moment the hunters may come upon
game of much more serious quality—lion or
buffalo; so that no one cares to be more than
a few yards from his heavy rifle or give his
mind wholly to the buck he stalks. Surely
they are perverse, unenterprising folk who
spend fortunes each year in preserving with
so much artificial care, and to the inconvenience of other dwellers in a small island,
well-counted herds of more or less tame deer,
when in a month, and for less expense than
the year's rent of their forests, they could
pursue wild animals of every kind in their
natural haunts and gain experiences that would
last them all their lives.

I was so much elated by this jolly morning's
sport and the near approach of civilized conditions—for after all, contrast is an element in
pleasure—that I permitted myself to rejoice
at the safe and happy outcome of this long
journey, and to exult in our complete immu-
nity from serious accident or illness or even
fever. How extravagant were the accounts
of the dangers of African travel! How easy to

avoid the evil chances of the road! Reasonable precautions, steady exercise, regular quinine—were these not in themselves the guarantees of safety? Thus I reckoned, and with specious reasons, but in a bad hour. We were not yet at our journey's end.

Twenty-four hours' steaming from Meshra-er-Zeraf brought us near Khartoum. The character of the country was unchanged. Yellow sand-slopes drank at the Nile brim; thorn-scrub fringed the river on either side; but date-palms mingled even more frequently and numerously with the vegetation, and brown mud-built villages with brown mud-coloured populations multiplied as the miles slipped swiftly by. At length a solitary majestic tree, beneath whose spacious branches and luxuriant foliage a hundred persons might have found shelter from the relentless sun—Gordon's tree—advertised us of the proximity of Khartoum. Soon on the one bank came into view the vast mud labyrinth of Omdurman, with forests of masts rising along the shore, and on the other, among palm-groves ever clustering thicker, sprang the blue and pink and crimson minarets of new Khartoum. Khartoum—the new Khartoum, risen from its ruins in wealth and beauty

THE PALACE, KHARTOUM.

P. 204.

—a smiling city sitting like a queen throned at the confluence of the Niles, the heart and centre of a far-reaching and formidable authority, disclosed herself to the traveller's eye. Sharp to the right turns the steamer, leaving the dull placid waters of the sovereign river we have so long followed, and shouldering a more turbulent current of clearer water, swings up-stream along its noble feudatory, the Blue Nile. And passing by the side of high stone embankments crowned by palms, the steamer enters into a modern Oriental port and city, and is soon surrounded by its palaces, its mosques, its warehouses and its quays.

Nearly ten years have passed since the Dervish domination was irretrievably shattered on the field of Omdurman, and every year has been attended by steady and remarkable progress in every sphere of governmental activity in every province of the Soudan. Order has been established, and is successfully, though precariously, maintained even in the remotest parts of Kordofan. The railway has reached the Southern bank of the Blue Nile, connects Khartoum with Cairo and with the Red Sea, waits only for the construction of a bridge to cross the river and enter the fertile

regions of the Ghezireh.   A numerous fleet of
steamers maintains swift and regular communication along the great waterways.   The revenue
has risen from a few thousands a year in 1899
to considerably over a million pounds in 1907.
Improved methods of agriculture have increased the wealth of the country; the prevention of massacre and famine has begun
to restore its population.   Slavery has been
abolished, and without affronting the religion
or seriously disturbing the customs of the
people, a measure of education and crafts-
manship has been introduced.

These great changes which are apparent
throughout the whole Soudan are nowhere
presented in so striking and impressive form
as in the capital.   A spacious palace, standing
in a beautiful garden, has risen from the ruins
where Gordon perished.   Broad thoroughfares
lighted by electricity, and lined with excellent
European shops, lead with geometrical precision
through the city.   A system of steam tramways
in connection with ferry boats, patronized chiefly
by the natives, renders communication easy
throughout Khartoum, and between Khartoum,
Omdurman, and Halfyah.   A semi-circle of
substantial barracks, arranged upon a defensive

GEORGE SCRIVINGS.   P. 207.

scheme, protects the landward approaches. The Gordon College hums with scholarly activity — Moslem and Christian, letters or crafts ; and seven thousand soldiers of all dress march past the British and Egyptian flags on occasions of ceremony.

Yet neither these inspiring facts—the more impressive by contrast with my memories of ten years before—nor the gracious hospitality of the Sirdar—more responsible than any other man for the whole of this tremendous task of reconstruction and revival—were to prevent me from taking away a sombre impression of Khartoum. As our steamer approached the landing-stage I learned that my English servant, George Scrivings, had been taken suddenly ill, and found him in a condition of prostration with a strange blue colour under his skin. Good doctors were summoned. The hospital of Khartoum, with all its resources, was at hand. There appeared no reason to apprehend a fatal termination. But he had been seized by a violent internal inflammation, the result of eating some poisonous thing which we apparently had escaped, and died early next morning after fifteen hours' illness, with almost every symptom of Asiatic cholera.

Too soon, indeed, had I ventured to rejoice. Africa always claims its forfeits; and so the four white men who had started together from Mombasa returned but three to Cairo. A military interment involves the union of the two most impressive rituals in the world. The day after the Battle of Omdurman it fell to my lot to bury those soldiers of the 21st Lancers, who had died of their wounds during the night. Now after nine years, in very different circumstances, from the other end of Africa, I had come back to this grim place where so much blood has been shed, and again I found myself standing at an open grave, while the yellow glare of the departed sun still lingered over the desert, and the sound of funeral volleys broke its silence.

*　　*　　*　　*　　*

The remainder of our journey lay in tourist lands, and the comfortable sleeping-cars of the Desert Railway, and the pleasant passenger steamers of the Wady Halfa and Assouan reach soon carried us prosperously and uneventfully to Upper Egypt; and so to Cairo, London, and the rest.

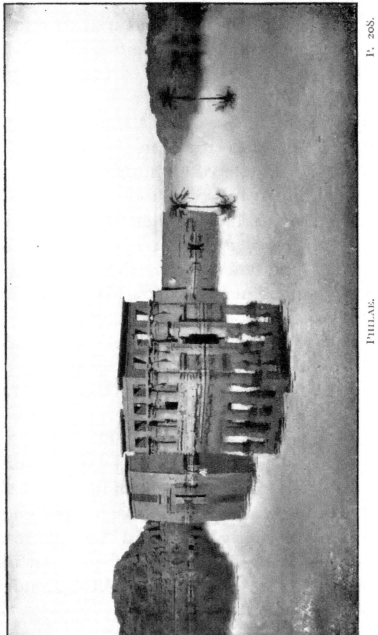

PHILAE.

CHAPTER XI

MY journey is at an end, the tale is told, and the reader who has followed so faithfully and so far has a right to ask what message I bring back. It can be stated in three words. Concentrate upon Uganda!

Over the greater part of the north-east quarter of Africa, British influence or authority in one form or another is supreme. But when I turn my mind over all those vast expanses, excluding only Egypt, there is no region which offers prospects to compare in hopefulness with those of the Protectorate of Uganda. The Soudan is far greater in extent and importance, and Great Britain is at no charge in respect to it. But the Soudan is clearly inferior in fertility. The East African Protectorate possesses not only enormous coast-lands of great value, but noble plateaux where the air is as cool as an English spring. But

we already spend on East Africa—and upon
the needs of its expensive white settlers—
more than the whole revenue of Uganda ; and
yet the promise is not so bright. Northern
Somaliland is a desert of rocks and thorn
bushes peopled by rifle-armed fanatics, on
which we spend nearly half as much as the
whole annual grant-in-aid of Uganda. And
between Somaliland and Uganda there is this
contrast presented in its crudest form—a barren
land with dangerous inhabitants ; and a fruitful
land with a docile people. What is least
worth having, is most difficult to hold : what
is most worth having, is easiest.

The union under scientific direction in
Uganda (and I include in this popular name
Usoga, Unyoro, Toro and Ankole, etc.) of un-
equalled fertility with a population of high
intelligence and social quality, in a region of
extraordinary waterways, must, unless some
grievous error or neglect should intervene,
result in remarkable economic developments.
Already more than half the traffic which passes
down the railway to Mombasa comes from
beyond the lake. Yet scarcely any money has
ever been spent on Uganda. No European
roads exist, no railways have been built, no

waterfalls are harnessed, no public works of any serious description have been undertaken. A poor little grant-in-aid has barely supported the day-to-day cost of European administration, and practically nothing in cash or credit has been available for the development of the country. But it is alive by itself. It is vital; and in my view, in spite of its insects and its diseases, it ought in the course of time to become the most prosperous of all our East and Central African possessions, and perhaps the financial driving wheel of all this part of the world. It is far from my desire to disparage the East African Protectorate, or to suggest diminution of activity or support. Both Protectorates are necessary to each other and should advance together; but in view of their relative positions, and looking at the situation as it is to-day, my counsel plainly is—" Concentrate upon Uganda ! " Nowhere else in Africa will a little money go so far. Nowhere else will the results be more brilliant, more substantial or more rapidly realized.

Cotton alone should make the fortune of Uganda. All the best qualities of cotton can be grown in the highest perfection, a hundred thousand intelligent landowners occupying twenty thousand square miles of suitable soil are eager to engage in the cultivation. An industrious and organized population offers the necessary labour. Merely at the request of the Government cotton has been planted experimentally on a considerable scale throughout Uganda. The figures of production—though of course they are only the first beginnings—show a surprising expansion. Great care is required, and steps have already been taken to secure that the quality of cotton exported from Uganda is not deteriorated or its reputation prejudiced by hasty or untutored action, that only the seeds which yield the best results should be distributed, and that no indiscriminate mixture should be permitted. ' The Government must control the culture. Experts must watch the ginneries and educate the native cultivator. Roads must be made to enable the crop to be marketed. The scientific organization of the cotton-growing resources of Uganda has now been definitely undertaken. A special grant of £10,000 a year will in future be devoted to this purpose, and the whole process will be supervised by European officers in close touch through the Colonial Office with the highest Manchester authorities and the British Cotton-Growing Association. In the opinion of the ablest observers the next five years will see a very remarkable development in cotton production, even though the means available to foster it continue to be slender.

But cotton is only one of those tropical products for which the demand of civilized industry is almost insatiable, and which can nowhere in the world be grown more cheaply, more easily, more perfectly than between the waters of the two great lakes. Rubber, fibre, cinnamon, cocoa, coffee, sugar may all be cultivated upon the greatest scale; virgin forests of rare and valuable timber await the axe; and even though mineral wealth may perhaps never lend its hectic glory to Uganda, the economic foundations of its prosperity will stand securely upon a rich and varied agriculture. A settler's country it can never be. Whatever may be the destinies of the East African Highlands, the shores of the great lakes will never be the permanent residence of a white race. It is a planter's land, where the labours of the native population may be organized and directed by superior intelligence and external capital. For my own part I rejoice that the physical conditions of the country are such as to prevent the growth in the heart of happy Uganda of a petty white community, with the harsh and selfish ideas which mark the jealous contact of races and the exploitation of the weaker.   Let it remain a "planter's land." Let the planters, instead of being the agents of excited syndicates with minds absorbed in the profits of shareholders thousands of miles away, be either Europeans of substance and character who have given proofs of their knowledge of natives and their ability to deal skilfully and justly with them, or better still— say I—let them be the disinterested officers of the Government, directing the development of the country neither in their own, nor any other pecuniary interest, but for the general good of its people and of the Empire of which it forms a part.

But if the immediate inflexion of British policy in Eastern Africa should be, without prejudice, but with precedence of other provinces, to accelerate the economic and social development of Uganda, what are the first steps to take ?   I might have much to say of Forestry and Agriculture ; of an extended system of technical education similar to that

given at the Gordon College at Khartoum, here
perhaps in part to be achieved through grants in
aid of the existing missionary schools ; of road-
making, indispensable to progress, of motor-
transport, and of water-power. But let me make
my message brief and unclouded, and as before
expressed in three words, " Build a Railway."

The clusters of colonial possessions which
have been acquired on the east and west coasts
of Africa, so rapidly and with so little cost or
bloodshed, will unquestionably prove an invalu-
able, if not indeed a necessary feature of the
British Empire. From these vast plantations
will be drawn the raw materials of many of
our most important industries ; to them will
flow a continuous and broadening train of
British products ; and in them the peculiar
gifts for administration and high civic virtues
of our race may find a healthy and an honourable scope. Some of these great estates, like
Southern Nigeria on the west coast, are already
so prosperous as not only to be self-supporting,
but able to assist with credit and subvention
the progress of neighbours less far advanced.
Others are still a charge upon our estimates.
We are annually put to the expense of grants-
in-aid more or less considerable for Northern

Somaliland, the East African Protectorate, Nyassaland and Uganda. Heavy upon the finance of all the East Coast hangs the capital charge of the Uganda Railway. In no way will these charges be eased or removed except by the rise of one or more of the territories concerned to economic buoyancy, or by the growth of railway traffic down the Uganda trunk consequent upon development. Under present conditions the progress made from year to year is steady and encouraging. The charges upon the Colonial Estimates diminish regularly every year. Every year the administration of the different Governments increases in elaboration, in efficiency and consequently in cost. The extra charge is met ever more fully by the returning yield of a grateful soil. Except for the chances of war, rebellion, pestilence, and famine which brood over the infancy of tropical protectorates, but which may be averted or controlled, it would be easy to calculate a date—not too remote—by which all contribution from the British tax-payer would be unnecessary. The movement of events is encouraging ; but there is one method by which it can be made far more sure and far more swift, by which all adverse chances are minimized, and all existing resources stimulated and multiplied—railways.

I would go so far as to say that it is only wasting time and money to try to govern, or still more develop, a great African possession without a railway. There can be no security, progress, or prosperity without at least one central line of rapid communication driven through the heart of the country. Where, as in Northern Somaliland, the land itself is utterly valueless, a mere desert of rocks and scrub, or where the military dangers are excessive and utterly disproportioned to any results that can ever be reaped—withdrawal and concentration are the true policy. But if for any reason it be decided to remain and to administer, a railway becomes the prime of absolute necessities. Till then all civilized government is extravagant and precarious, and all profitable commerce practically impossible. These considerations have lately led a British Government to sanction the extensive railways, nearly 600 miles long, now being rapidly constructed in Northern and Southern Nigeria; and the same arguments apply, though in my view with increased force, to the Uganda Protectorate.

It is not usually realized that the Uganda railway does not pass through Uganda.   It is the railway *to* Uganda and not *of* Uganda. It stops short of the land from which it takes its name, and falls exhausted by its exertions and vicissitudes, content feverishly to lap the waters of the Victoria Nyanza.   Uganda is reached, but not traversed by steam communication in any form.   Yet the extension of the railway from the western shores of the Victoria to the Albert Nyanza would not only carry it through much of the most valuable and fertile country within its radius, but as I shall show could far more than double its effective scope.

It may be accepted as an axiom that in the present state of development in these African protectorates, it is scarcely ever, and indeed I think never, worth while to build railways in competition with waterways.   Railways should in new countries be in supplement of, and not in substitution for, lakes and navigable rivers. No doubt direct through-routes of railway, where bulk is not broken and all delays and changings are avoided, show an imposing advantage in comparison with a mere alternation of water stages and railway links.   There could be no doubt which was the better if only you leave out the question of cost. But it is just this question of cost which cannot be left out, which clamorously dominates the proposition from the beginning. For first-class countries may afford first-class railways and *trains de luxe*, but second-class countries must be less ambitious, and young new jungle-born countries are satisfied, or ought to be, if they get any railway at all. The differences between the best railway in the world and the worst, are no doubt impressive ; but they become utterly insignificant when contrasted with the difference between the worst railway in the world and no railway at all. For observe, the comparison is not with perfect lines of European communication, nor with anything like them, nor even with a waggon on a turnpike road. It is with a jogging, grunting, panting, failing line of tottering coolies, men reduced to beasts of burden, that the new pioneer line must be compared—that is to say, with the most painful, most degrading, slowest and feeblest method of transportation which has ever disgraced the world. And compared with that, any line of steam-communication, however primitive, however light, however interrupted, is heaven.

I am endeavouring to guide the reader to a positive proposal of a modest and practical character, I mean the construction of a new railway which might be called "The Victoria and Albert Railway," although it would virtually be an extension of the existing Uganda line.   This railway should traverse the country between the great lakes, and join together these two noble reservoirs with all their respective river connections.   The distance is not great.   Two hundred and fifty miles would exceed the largest computation ; and perhaps a line of one hundred and fifty miles would suffice.   If the cost of this railway were estimated, as I am informed is reasonable, at a maximum figure of £5,000 a mile, the total sum involved would be between £1,250,000 and £750,000.

The supreme advantage of making a railway debouch upon a great lake, is that every point on the lake shore is instantly put in almost equal communication with railhead.   Steamers coast round on circular tours, and whatsoever trade or traffic may offer along the whole circumference, is carried swiftly to the railway. Lakes are in fact the catchment areas of trade, and it is by tapping and uniting them that the economic life of Central Africa can be most easily and swiftly stimulated.

Two routes present themselves with various competing advantages by which the Victoria and Albert Railway may proceed. The first, the most obvious, most desirable and most expensive, is straight across the Highlands of Toro, through the best of the cotton country, from a point on the Victoria Lake in the neighbourhood of Entebbe, to where the Semliki river runs into the southern end of Lake Albert. The second would practically follow the footsteps recorded in these pages. It does not offer a direct line. It does not pass during the whole of its length through cultivated and inhabited country. It does not reach the Albert Lake at the most convenient end. But it is far cheaper than the other. It is only 135 miles long instead of nearly 250. It connects not only the two great lakes, but also Lake Chioga with all its channels and tributaries, in one system of unbroken steam communication.

Briefly this latter project would consist of two links of railway: the first about sixty miles long from Jinja (or Ripon Falls) to Kakindu, the first point where the Victoria Nile becomes navigable : the second about seventy-five miles long from the neighbourhood of Mruli to the Nile below the Murchison Falls and near its mouth on the Albert.   By these two sections of railway, together only 135 miles in length, a wonderful extent of waterways would be commanded; to wit : 1. Thirty miles of the Victoria Nile navigable from Kakindu to Lake Chioga.   2. Lake Chioga itself, with its long arms and gulfs stretching deeply into the whole of the fertile regions to the south-west of Mount Elgon, and affording a perimeter of navigable coastline accessible by steamers, of certainly not less than 250 miles.   3. All that reach of the Victoria Nile navigable from Lake Chioga to Foweira when the rapids ending in the Murchison Falls begin again—70 miles. 4. Thirty miles from below the falls to the Albert Lake. 5. The whole of the Albert Lake shores—250 miles.   6. The Semliki river navigable (once a sandbar has been passed) for sixty miles. 7. The glorious open reach of the White Nile from the Albert Lake to Nimule—120 miles.   Thus by the construction of only 135 miles of railroad, swift modern communication would be established over a total range of 800 miles: or for an addition of one-fifth to its length and one-eighth to its cost the effective radius of the Uganda railway would be more than doubled. Such railway propositions are few and far between.

I do not prejudge the choice of these two routes. Both are now being carefully surveyed. The advantages of the longer and more ambitious line across Toro are perhaps superior. But the cost is also nearly twice as great ; and cost is a vital factor—not merely to the government called upon to find money, but still more to the commercial soundness of an enterprise which is permanently crippled, if its original capital charges are allowed notably to exceed what the estimated earnings would sustain. The question is one which will require severe and patient examination, the nicest balancings between competitive advantages, the smoothest compromises between the practical and the ideal.

But let us now look forward to a time—not, I trust, remote—when by one route or the other the distance between the Victoria and Albert Lakes has been spanned by a railway, and when the Mountains of the Moon are scarcely four days' journey from Mombasa. The British Government will then be possessed of the shortest route to the Eastern Congo. The Uganda railway will be able to offer rates for merchandise and railway material with which no other line that can ever be constructed will ever be able to compete. The whole of that already considerable, though as yet stifled trade, which feebly trickles back half across Africa by Boma to the Atlantic, which is looking desperately for an outlet to the northward, which percolates in driblets through Uganda to-day, will flow swiftly and abundantly to the benefit of all parties concerned down the Uganda trunk, raising that line with steady impulse from the *status* of a political railway towards the level of a sound commercial enterprise. In no other way will the British tax-payer recover his capital. The advantages are great and the expense moderate. Larger considerations may postpone, and the imperative need of the fullest surveys will in any case delay construction ; but I cannot doubt that the Victoria and Albert railway is now the most important project awaiting action in the whole of that group of Protectorates which Sir Frederick Lugard used proudly to call " our East African Empire."

But let us proceed one step further in the

development of the communications of north-east Africa. When an extension of the Uganda railway has reached the Albert Nyanza, only one link will be missing to connect the whole of the rail and waterway system of East Africa and Uganda with the enormous system of railways and riverways of Egypt and the Soudan, to connect the Uganda with the Desert railway, to join the navigation of the great lakes to the navigation of the Blue and White Niles. Only one link will be missing, and that a very short one; the distance of 110 miles from Nimule to Gondokoro, where the Nile is interrupted by cataracts. Of the commercial utility of such a link *in itself* I have nothing to say; but as a means of marrying two gigantic systems of steam communication, it will some day possess a high importance; and thereafter over the whole of the north-east quarter of the African continent under the influence or authority of the British Crown, comprising a total mileage by rail and river of perhaps 20,000 miles, uninterrupted steam communication will prevail.

The adventurous and the imaginative may peer out beyond these compact and practicable steps into a more remote and speculative region.

15

Perhaps by the time that the junction between the Uganda and Soudan rail and water systems has been effected, the Rhodes Cape to Cairo railway will have reached the southern end of Lake Tanganyika : and then only one comparatively short hiatus will bar a complete transcontinental line, if not wholly of railroad, at least of steam traffic and of comfortable and speedy travel.

Then, perhaps it will be time to make another journey ; but as the reader, who will no doubt take care to secure a first-class tourist ticket, will no longer require my services as guide, I shall take this opportunity of making him my bow.

THE END

ImTheStory.com

Personalized Classic Books in many genre's

Unique gift for kids, partners, friends, colleagues

Customize:

- Character Names
- Upload your own front/back cover images (optional)
- Inscribe a personal message/dedication on the
  inside page (optional)

Customize many titles Including
- Alice in Wonderland
- Romeo and Juliet
- The Wizard of Oz
- A Christmas Carol
- Dracula
- Dr. Jekyll & Mr. Hyde
- And more...

This book is dedicated to the memory of my good friend and former colleague Jim Page. His 30-plus years of commitment and dedicated service to the Illinois Department of Corrections will forever be appreciated and remembered.

Cover and Interior Design by Imagine! Studios, LLC
www.ArtsImagine.com

Published by Linguistic Freedom Publications
Greensboro, NC

Articles appearing in the Appendices were previously published and are reprinted with permission from their orignial publishers.

ISBN 13: 978-0-9895873-0-3

Library of Congress Control Number: 2013911669

First Linguistic Freedom Publications printing: July 2013

The Anatomy of
PRISON LIFE

Behind the Walls
of the Illinois
Department of
Corrections

CHARLES L. HINSLEY

Linguistic Freedom Publications
Greensboro, NC

THE ANATOMY OF
PRISON LIFE

Praise for *The Anatomy of Prison Life*

"Just got through the first chapter . . . I am hooked!"

—Christina Calabria, Social Advocate

"Just read first chapter. Riveting!!!"

—Jan Prichett, Attorney at Law

"I just finished reading your book. I asked for the *truth* of prison life, and you give it in all of its unadulterated form—straight with no chaser. I will tell anyone who wants to know what it is truly like to be in prison, to read your book!"

—Thomas Rush, writer and author

"As it pertains to the IL DOC it is insightful and factually true as it corresponds with my personal experience between the years 1991 and 2000."

—Herman Moore, former chaplain in Illinois Department of Corrections

"I could not help but think of one word: Suburb!!!

—Richard Vance, from a perspective of personal experience

"Interesting, informative, and fascinating!

—Anita Francois, a professional clinical social worker

CPSIA information can be obtained at www.ICGtesting.com
Printed in the USA
BVOW06s1202211015

423459BV00010B/103/P